THE INNOCENCE OF MEMORIES

ORHAN PAMUK
The Innocence of Memories

Translated by Ekin Oklap

FABER & FABER

First published in the UK in 2018
by Faber & Faber Limited
Bloomsbury House
74–77 Great Russell Street
London WC1B 3DA
Originally published in Turkey by Yapi Kredi Yayinlari in 2016

Typeset by Ian Bahrami
Printed and bound in India by Replika Press Pvt. Ltd.

*INNOCENCE OF MEMORIES, ORHAN PAMUK'S
MUSEUM & ISTANBUL*
A Film by GRANT GEE,
Produced by JANINE MARMOT and KEITH GRIFFITHS
The Film was made with support from the BFI and BORD SCANNÁN na
hÉIREANN/THE IRISH FILM BOARD,
a HOT PROPERTY PRODUCTION
in co-production with ILLUMINATIONS FILMS, VENOM, IN
BETWEEN ART FILM and VIVO FILM and in association with FINITE
FILMS and ARTE FRANCE–LA LUCARNE

A CIP record for this book
is available from the British Library

ISBN 978–0–571–33866–5

2 4 6 8 10 9 7 5 3 1

Contents

A Novel and a Museum Are the Same Thing

I wrote the novel while thinking of the museum, and created the museum while thinking of the novel. The museum was not just some idea I chanced upon after the success of the book, nor was it a case of the success of the museum begetting the novel, like the book version of some blockbuster film. In fact, I conceived the book and the museum simultaneously, and explained their intricate connection in the novel: a young man from a wealthy, westernised Istanbul family falls in love with a poor distant relation, and when his love goes unrequited, he finds solace in collecting everything his beloved has ever touched. Finally, as we learn at the end of the novel, he takes all of these everyday objects he has accumulated – postcards, photographs, matchsticks, saltshakers, keys, dresses, film clips, and toys, mementoes of his doomed love affair and of the Istanbul of the 1970s and 1980s whose streets he wandered with his lover – and puts them on display in Istanbul's Museum of Innocence.

Back in the mid-nineties, when I first embarked on this artistic and literary project, my dream was to open the museum on the same day the novel was published. I would arrange the chapters in meticulous order, producing a museum catalogue that could be read as a novel – a postmodern sort of novel. But I finished the book before the museum, recasting it into the form of a traditional novel, without images or annotations, and published it in 2008.

When I opened the museum in 2012, I realised I still needed an actual museum catalogue to explain the design and composition of the exhibition vitrines I had so painstakingly devised, and to showcase the objects and photographs in the collection, so I wrote *The Innocence of Objects*.

Now, there is a fourth work, one which I'd never imagined when I first embarked on this project: Grant Gee's beautiful, enigmatic documentary film *Innocence of Memories*. This time I'm not the creative force behind the work; instead, my role is that of creator of the film's focus, the Museum of Innocence, and author of the texts featured in the film.

It all started when Grant Gee came to Istanbul for a screening of his ingenious film on W. G. Sebald's *The Rings of Saturn*. When I found out that Grant was interested in shooting a documentary about the Museum of Innocence, I was eager to get involved on the creative side. We met up in London, and talked for hours. Then we met up in Istanbul, and walked for miles. Was it Grant who asked, 'Is there anywhere in Istanbul that means something special to you?' or was it my idea to 'show him around'? I can't remember now. Perhaps we weren't aiming for anywhere in particular, but hoping that our footsteps would help us to penetrate the emotional fabric of the city.

I ended up with conflicting feelings. As we roamed the streets, I was remembering a past that had been quietly fading away, and trying at the same time to work out which of the many things we saw might interest anyone other than me. Strolling through Istanbul with someone who was a stranger to the city I'd lived in my whole life lent me a different perspective on that life, on the city, and on my memories. When we come across something beautiful or interesting, how much of that is the city itself, and how much of it is our own nostalgia? How beautiful or how interesting can a city be without the benefit of our memories? And when buildings, bridges, and squares are demolished, are our memories erased and eroded with them?

Innocence of Memories is based as much on the novel as it is on the objects that inspired it (clocks, coffee cups, photographs, clips from old movies set in Istanbul), on daydreams lyrically layered, and on the actual landscape of the city. The camera's focus on the streets where I found the objects for my collection befits my vision of what museums should be: the future of museums is in our homes, in our daily lives, and on the streets. Museums should no longer concern themselves with state histories, the sagas of kings and heroes, or the forging of national identities; they should focus instead on the lives and belongings of ordinary people, just as modern novels do. When I began to prepare for the novel and the museum, walking around the streets of Istanbul, raiding flea markets, second-hand bookstores, and the homes of friends and family for old pillboxes, ashtrays, framed pictures of mosques, identity cards, and passport photos, I realised that collecting artefacts for a museum is not very different from collecting stories and facts for a novel.

The love story in *The Museum of Innocence* takes place primarily between 1974 and 1980, while the museum features objects and images used and seen by the people of Istanbul and the characters in the novel across the second half of the twentieth century. But Grant's curious camera was equally interested in the twenty-first-century city, the rapid, vicious urbanisation and accumulation of wealth that had taken place over the past fifteen years, and how the city's new

ix

skyscrapers now coexisted with its older, melancholy soul. What could we do?

The protagonists of our unhappy love story had died, and the house they'd lived in had been converted into a museum. So I turned to a character who'd only had a minor role in the novel but nevertheless remembered the love affair clearly: Ayla. I imagined that she had left Istanbul for political reasons shortly after the time of the novel, only to find upon her return twelve years later that her city had been transformed. Just like me and Grant Gee, Ayla would go on long walks through the streets of Istanbul, while I happily transcribed her thoughts on the city, memory, and life.

This film, like the novel and museum, stems mostly from my endless wanderings in Istanbul. In the second half of the 1990s, I combed through the streets and neighbourhoods of the city centre in search of a building (that I could afford to buy) where the protagonists of my imaginary love story could live, and which I could later convert into a museum. (Houses and land were cheap back then, and there weren't as many tourists around.) In 1998, I bought the first piece of my collection, the 120-year-old building in Çukurcuma which now hosts the museum. I kept walking, searching for old crockery, kitchen utensils, liquor bottles, keys, clocks, cigarette holders, and photographs of everyday scenes that would have been part of the lives of the invented characters who had lived in that building. (Istanbul's flea markets, second-hand bookshops, and increasingly popular collectors of everyday paraphernalia hadn't yet embraced the internet.) I began writing a new novel called *A Strangeness in My Mind* around the time that I was setting up the museum, and went on long night-time walks around the poorer neighbourhoods that stood at the heart of the city and were home to the hero of this new novel, a street vendor. Sometimes I would stay in my writing studio working on this novel until four in the morning, and I loved walking back home through those night-time streets shrouded in darkness and silence. In our long walks with Grant through some of the city's more deprived, dangerous, remote, and crumbling neighbourhoods, we saw the same dogs that have been ruling the streets at night since Ottoman times. Their packs had perhaps disbanded, but lone dogs still padded patiently down the infinite streets of the city, and keenly observed our progress. On our walks, we seldom spoke; much like Grant's camera in *Innocence of Memories*, we concentrated only on the emotions evoked by the city's darkened nooks, its ruins and shadows. Maybe that's why Grant never asked me the question everyone else always does: 'Why did you decide to create this museum when you'd already written the novel?' Had he asked, I wouldn't have given him my usual answer: 'I was possessed by a jinn.' Nor would I have told him, 'When I was younger, I wanted to be a painter.' Instead, I would have said, 'Perhaps a novel and a museum are more or less the same thing.'

INNOCENCE OF MEMORIES

(*Screenplay*)

Fırın'ün Masuniyet Mü...
...mı hahrladığı...
...itile vcire...
...ller ae d...
...l ile e...

AYLA: As soon as I saw Füsun's dress in the Museum of Innocence, I remembered it. We had bought it together, cheaply, in a backstreet in Beyoğlu.

My name is Ayla. Füsun was my friend. I was her neighbour for eleven years. From 1974 to 1985, we were her father Tarık Bey's ground-floor tenants. Later, I got married and went to live in Beşiktaş. My husband is an electrical engineer. He joined the electrical engineers' union and got mixed up in politics. He was put under investigation. We had our children to think of, so when the rumour spread that they were going to start arresting people, we fled to Bremen in Germany. We didn't come back for twelve years.

When I returned to Istanbul in 2013, twelve years later, I found that the city had changed completely. Getting to know your own city all over again is like making new memories. But all I did was search for my old ones.

That's how I ended up in Çukurcuma, the neighbourhood where Füsun used to live. It was early evening but already dark, and there, in front of me, was our old house. The same building where Füsun had lived on the floor above us, with her mother Nesibe and her father Tarık, was now a museum: the Museum of Innocence. Its main entrance was the same door that once used to lead into the apartment we rented. They were selling tickets at the door, and the usual silence of museums reigned inside.

INNOCENCE OF MEMORIES

ORHAN PAMUK AUDIO GUIDE: Welcome to the Museum of Innocence. This is Orhan Pamuk. This audio guide has been prepared to guide you through our museum. I will also read some extracts from my novel *The Museum*

of Innocence. The novel, beginning in 1974, tells the story of protagonist Kemal's love for his distant relative, Füsun. After Füsun marries someone else, Kemal continues to visit her for nine years here in this house, now turned into a museum, and collects everything that reminds him of his beloved.

AYLA: I knew there was a novel about Füsun. I was one of the people Orhan Pamuk spoke to while he was writing it. I've read the book: in fact, I'm in it. I'm there as one of Füsun's friends, one of those people who told him her story. He gets the two of us mixed up in some parts, which doesn't surprise me at all. Towards the end of the 1970s and in the days following the coup in 1980, Füsun and I were inseparable.

ORHAN PAMUK AUDIO GUIDE: The Museum of Innocence has five floors. The Keskin family lived on the first and second floors of this building between 1974 and 1999. Now please walk up the stairs ahead of you to reach the first box, which corresponds to the first chapter of the novel. I wish you a happy and enjoyable visit.

KEMAL: It was the happiest moment of my life, though I didn't know it. Had I known, had I cherished this gift, would everything have turned out differently? Yes, if I had recognised this instant of perfect happiness, I would have held it fast and never let it slip away. It took a few seconds, perhaps,

for that luminous state to enfold me, suffusing me with the deepest peace, but it seemed to last hours, even years. In that moment, on the afternoon of Monday May 26th, 1975, at about quarter to three, just as we felt ourselves to be beyond sin and guilt, so too did the world seem to have been released from gravity and time.

When we met the next day, Füsun told me she had lost one of her earrings.

AYLA: I read that the love story started like this. Kemal's fiancée Sibel happened to spot a designer handbag in the window of the Şanzelize Boutique and casually mentioned how much she liked it. And I read that later, to surprise her, a month away from their engagement party, Kemal returned alone to buy the bag. The shop assistant who served him was Füsun. As soon as he saw her Kemal felt his heart in his throat with the force of an immense wave about to crash against the shore. And I read that Kemal watched as Füsun retrieved the handbag from the shop window and slipped off her yellow high-heeled pump, extending a bare foot whose nails she'd carefully painted red. And I read that though it wasn't even May yet, her long, bare legs were already tanned. At least, that's how Kemal told it to Orhan Pamuk.

INTERVIEW, EMRE AYVAZ: Orhan Pamuk is a Turkish novelist, born in Istanbul in 1952. He has been writing novels in the city for forty years. He has had nine novels published

so far, and ever since his books began to be translated into foreign languages, he has become known throughout the world as a writer of Istanbul, particularly through his novels *The Black Book*, *My Name is Red*, and *The Museum of Innocence*, published respectively in 1990, 1998, and 2008. In 2006, Orhan Pamuk was awarded the Nobel Prize for Literature. His latest novel, *A Strangeness in My Mind*, was published in 2014. His Museum of Innocence, which shares the same name as the title of his previous novel, opened in Istanbul in 2012.

INTERVIEW, ORHAN PAMUK: I wanted readers of the novel to know that the objects described in the book and used by its characters were also displayed in an actual museum. Ideally, readers of *The Museum of Innocence* should know that there is a museum of that name, and visitors to the Museum of Innocence should know that there is a corresponding novel. But I've also met readers who've never seen the museum. Some people think the museum is some sort of Borgesian joke. Conversely, around 50 per cent or 60 per cent of visitors to the museum are people who haven't read the book. They have a different perspective; they come in search of a quirky cultural experience.

AYLA: When I came back to the city after twelve years, the Museum of Innocence was the place where I felt most at home . . . Every time I came back to it, I discovered a little bit more about the magic of ordinary objects. Perhaps all our homes are museums, really.

INTERVIEW, ORHAN PAMUK: I first had the idea for the Museum of Innocence in the mid-nineties. My books were getting translated into foreign languages, and I often travelled to Europe for festivals, book launches, and talks. I was curious about Europe, and I used my spare time during

those trips to see as many museums as I could, large or small. In this way I began to appreciate smaller museums, seeing how similar they were to novels. You can go to the Louvre for a comprehensive history of French art, but the Edith Piaf Museum in Paris will enable you to experience 1950s France through the life of a single person. My enthusiasms can be sudden and variable, and soon I had made up my mind: 'I'll set up my own little museum.' I didn't have the money to pay for it, but I was determined. Then I began to plan an experimental novel. It would be structured in such a way that its publication would naturally complement the museum.

AYLA: At the start of the affair in May 1975, Füsun was just eighteen, a poor distant relation. At the end, August 28th, 1984, she was twenty-seven. She and Kemal made love forty-four times. She had honey-hued arms and quick, elegant gestures. She smiled the well-measured smile of

well-mannered beauties accustomed to compliments. She swam gracefully and very fast. Sometimes she would assume a little girl's expression. She would go by herself to paint birds. She blushed. She would sulk. She yawned so beautifully. She told him that when they first made love, she was imagining a field of sunflowers. Kemal was thirty-one when he met Füsun, thirteen years older, almost a different generation. Perhaps this explains his first and maybe fundamental mistake. He told Füsun that she was modern and courageous to give him her virginity. I suppose he meant it as a compliment, but to her it would have meant that he would feel no special obligations to her just because she'd slept with him, and that if she was 'modern', she would not see sex with a man before marriage as a burden, and neither would she worry about being a virgin on her wedding day. She would, in fact, be just like those European women that men like Kemal entertained in their fantasies. It's difficult to believe how important these ways of thinking were back then. And I read that even though he and Füsun met every day in secret and made love for hours at a time with ever-increasing abandon, Kemal never asked himself what allowed him to feel such pleasure with her. He told Orhan Pamuk that he behaved only like a child greedily gulping one sweet after another.

KEMAL: If the man tried to wriggle out of marrying the girl he slept with, and the girl in question was under eighteen years of age, an angry father might take the philanderer to court to force him to marry her. Some such cases would attract press attention, and in those days it was the custom for newspapers to run photographs with black bands over

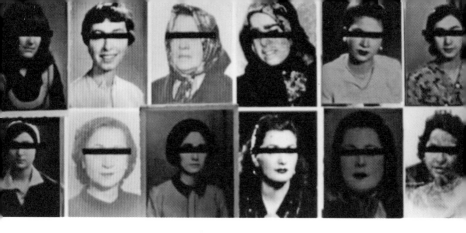

the 'violated' girls' eyes, to spare their being identified in this shameful situation. Because the press used the same device in photographs of adulteresses, rape victims, and prostitutes, there were so many photographs of women with black bands over their eyes that to read a Turkish newspaper in those days was like wandering through a masquerade. All in all, Turkish newspapers ran very few photographs of Turkish women without bands over their eyes, unless they were singers, actresses, or beauty contestants (all occupations suggestive of easy virtue, anyway), while in advertisements there was a preference for women and faces that were evidently foreign and non-Muslim.

AYLA: I was starting to get used to the city again, twelve years after I'd left. It felt like I was discovering it afresh, finding backstreets and distant neighbourhoods which hadn't changed at all or at least felt no different, and those pavements and ancient streets where only shadows moved at night.

INTERVIEW, ORHAN PAMUK: I love the idea of a person wandering the city, looking for signs. My novels are partly influenced by the noir genre, and so-called B-movies. You have someone telling a story. The story may be crude and

far-fetched, but what matters, in my view, is the crumbling city, its vistas and hidden details – its tumultuous essence. My Istanbul is not a place you can display in a museum. It is a neglected city, where everything is mixed up with everything else. Everything there is old. Everything is worn out. There is a fixed idea, an image in my mind of a lone figure searching for something in these dilapidated surroundings. That's another reason why I love walking in the city in the middle of the night.

AYLA: Istanbul at night. A population of men and dogs. The city connected all night, every night, by thousands of yellow taxis in mysterious orbits, each an indivisible atom, but together seeming to trace a single secret meaning on the city.

TAXI DRIVER: I've been a taxi driver for twenty-eight years. Istanbul is prettier at night, when all the day's filth is covered up. There is a beauty in the city then that hides everything that happens during the day. You know, Istanbul during the day is harder to live in than anywhere else in this country. I've seen about three quarters of Turkey. There's hardly a city, town, or village I haven't seen. Three quarters, I've seen, though I guess not all of it. But this I know: you will have no trouble during the daytime anywhere else. Here in Istanbul you don't find that tranquillity. It's very different here, during the day.

AYLA: There is no daylight in the Museum of Innocence. It feels like night and dreaming. Perhaps this is why it was so easy for me to feel at home there. Once, I found myself staring with a powerful sense of déjà vu at a photograph of a *salep* vendor on the Galata Bridge at night. It took me a while to realise that, like many of the other photographs in the museum, it is by Ara Güler. Like all *Istanbullus* of my generation, I have seen some of his photographs so many times that I confuse them with my own memories of the city.

ARA GÜLER: I am Ara Güler. I was born in 1928 in this city called Istanbul. So, if you count from 1928, I must be around eighty-five now. All these years, I've been watching Istanbul. If you look at my photographs today, you'll find my memories in them. Whatever we do, we can never get away from our memories. I must have taken two million photographs, maybe more . . . I have no idea, I don't remember, I never counted. See this building? It belonged to my father. It's been there since before I was born. I can't say when exactly, but one day, this building is going to be a museum. It will be the museum of my foundation. My archives will be in proper

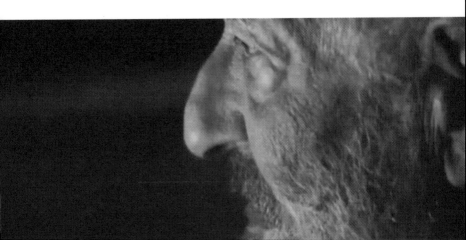

order then. But I don't know when it will be. Perhaps I'll die before it happens. But I don't mind, you know?

AYLA: And now, I can't tell whether I like Ara Güler's photographs because they remind me of what Istanbul was like when I was a child, or because they're simply beautiful. But maybe beauty and memory are not separate things. Love is familiar. In the *Museum of Innocence* I read that while Kemal was not yet using the word 'love' to describe his feelings for Füsun, he had begun to suffer its first symptoms. He was already worried that he was becoming besotted, and he already felt intense jealousy when he realised that the sexual pleasure that Füsun had discovered with him could now

also be experienced with other men. And on the day that was to contain the happiest moment of his life, Kemal, wracked with jealousy when Füsun was just ten minutes late for their rendezvous, ran out into the streets of Nişantaşı and found her as she was approaching the apartments.

KEMAL: As we walked without speaking up the street where the police station was, straight to the Merhamet Apartments, we were fast approaching the 'happiest moment of my life' mentioned at the beginning of my book.

With our heads on the pillow, our view was of the radiator pipe, the lidded hole for the stovepipe, the window cornice, the curtains, the lines and corners where the walls met the ceiling, the cracks in the wall, the peeling paint, and the layer of dust.

AYLA: Sometimes it was difficult for me to read the novel, in particular to read about the intimate details of Füsun and Kemal's lovemaking. We never talked about such things. But now I, and anybody who reads even just the first page of the novel, knows that the happiest moment of Kemal's life occurred just as he 'gently entered Füsun' and that this was also the precise moment that her earring came loose and fell. Sometimes, reading the novel felt like reading a diary that I shouldn't have seen, and somehow, discovering these secrets from Füsun's past changes my past, too.

KEMAL: Afterwards, Füsun looked into my eyes. 'My whole life depends on you now,' she said in a low voice. This both pleased and alarmed me.

AYLA: I read that Kemal and Füsun continued to meet and make love every day, right up to the day of Kemal and Sibel's engagement party. Even on the actual day of Kemal and Sibel's engagement party. And I read that as he watched Füsun leave the Merhamet Apartments that day, just a few hours before it was due to begin, Kemal knew that his engagement party would be a great success. In the Museum of Innocence, Füsun's socks, sneakers, and underwear are displayed alongside the invitation to Kemal and Sibel's party on the Bosphorus Terrace of the Hilton Hotel.

INTERVIEW, ORHAN PAMUK: I was a child when the Hilton first opened its doors. Every visit there was an event. The people of Nişantaşı loved going to the Hilton; it made them feel more American, more European. I would go with them. All parties, including the engagement party in *The Museum of Innocence*, were thrown at the Hilton. The first time I ever ate a hamburger was at the Hilton. There were some dances I learned, some films I watched for the first time at the Hilton. The Hilton, where the West made its first inroads into Turkey, where Turkish people first encountered the concept of westernisation, and western-ers first encountered Istanbul, was such an important place that all the major national newspapers used to have Hilton correspondents.

AYLA: Füsun made a big mistake in going to Kemal and Sibel's expensive engagement party at the Hilton. She told me herself over and over again that she'd made a mistake. She was meant to take her university entrance exams the next day. She was trying to pretend everything was normal. Going to that party, having to stand among that gathering of happy, wealthy guests and watch Kemal get engaged to another girl made her heartbreak harder to bear, and she fell ill. I wasn't invited to Kemal's engagement party, of course. All I know about it is what Orhan Pamuk wrote in his book. Füsun never liked to talk about the Hilton Hotel. Orhan Pamuk danced with her at the party, and maybe that's where he got the emotional motivation needed to write this long novel and set up a museum with Kemal.

INTERVIEW, ORHAN PAMUK: Füsun was exactly like Ayla describes her. When I saw her for the first time at the engagement party at the Hilton, I had no idea she would become the protagonist of my novel . . . I was an awkward, restless young man back then. I danced with her because she was beautiful, but she wasn't all that interested in me. I wasn't particularly handsome, anyway. Later, I found out more about Füsun through Kemal's story. After Kemal died, I sought out Ayla and others who knew Füsun in order to write my novel. I always research all my books. I did everything I could to bring Füsun to life, to make her real.

AYLA: Curiosity took me back to the Hilton, and I found that everything around it had changed. And while the staircases, the function halls, and the rooms may have stayed the same, the atmosphere they evoked had changed completely. Those places which had once had such an effect on Füsun, Kemal, and Orhan had now become unremarkable city spaces. The only thing that remained the same was the view of the Bosphorus, and the Cityline ferries as they made their nightly journeys back to dock . . .

FERRY WORKER: I prefer working nights, when everything

is calmer. When there's no traffic on the Bosphorus . . . When there are no fishermen, no motor boats, our job is simpler and safer. And people, people at night, tend to be more reasonable. Most of them are tired after a day at work, maybe they're on their way home. So that's why it's always easier at night. There are so many kinds of currents from one end of the Bosphorus to the other. There are lots of turns, too; it isn't a straight passage. That also has an effect. There is a current that goes from the Black Sea to the Marmara Sea, and one in the opposite direction, towards the Black Sea. When the *lodos* wind blows, the currents flow a certain way; when the north-easterly *poyraz* blows, they change direction and strength. I've seen with my own eyes how certain boats, the kind we call 'sinkers', get swept back before they can sail past the Maiden's Tower. There's a powerful current by the Sarayburnu promontory that takes you all the way to the Marmara Sea. Cross over to the other side, to Kabataş, and the current will take you back towards Beşiktaş. There are currents and counter-currents everywhere. Back in the day, sailboats used to follow the coastline on the European side up to a point and then cross over to the Asian side to avoid the currents.

AYLA: I read that, in the weeks following his engagement party, Kemal would still go to the Merhamet Apartments to wait for Füsun to come. Every day, at ten minutes to two, he would take out the key with trembling hands and let himself in, joyfully believing that in ten or fifteen minutes, Füsun would arrive and they would be making love.

KEMAL: Every day I went to the Merhamet Apartments at the customary hour, to begin my wait. Having realised that getting there early only aggravated my pain, I resolved not to arrive before five minutes to two. I would go into the apartment trembling with impatience, and during the first ten or fifteen minutes hopeful anticipation would ease the pain, an excitement wreathing my head down to the tip of my nose even as my heart ached and my stomach cramped.

This depiction of the internal organs of the human body is taken from an advertisement for Paradison, a painkiller on display in the window of every pharmacy in Istanbul at the time, and I use it here to illustrate to the museum visitor where the agony of love first appeared, where it became most pronounced, and how far it spread.

One: where the deepest pain is initially felt.

Two: as the pain increases, it will radiate to the cavity between the lungs and the stomach. At that point its abdominal presence will no longer be confined to the left side, as it will have spread to the right.

Three: you will feel as if a hot poker or a screwdriver were twisting into you.

Four: it is as if the stomach and then the entire abdomen were filling up with acid.

Five: it is as if sticky, red-hot little starfish were attaching themselves to your organs.

Six: the pain of jealousy is initially felt in the mind and soon triggers a pain in the stomach, bringing the lover to devastation.

AYLA: Listening to the anatomy of Kemal's melancholy was like discovering the science of *hüzün*, Turkish melancholy, in the streets of Istanbul. Looking at the city now, it's sometimes difficult to remember that when we were growing up, we felt that we were living in a black-and-white world, the ruins of the Ottoman Empire.

INTERVIEW, ORHAN PAMUK: The beautiful city views that Istanbul gifts us, the feel of the streets at midnight when the dogs take over, the city's dilapidated backstreets, its cemeteries, its moss-covered walls, its old wooden homes with crooked bay windows, its new concrete buildings with their plaster already crumbling, its muddy, wood-coloured, unadorned streets, its cobbled pavements, all of these things together inject a feeling of *hüzün* into the inhabitants of Istanbul. This, I have determined, is the fundamental feeling the city conveys. But this idea of 'Turkish melancholy', *hüzün*, also comes with a philosophical aspect: it is a warning against success and wealth. The philosophy of *hüzün* seems to tell us, 'Don't you dare be successful in life. Don't you dare try to marry the girl you love. You will fail.' It is about favouring humility over success. The philosophy of *hüzün* tells us, 'Retreat into your shell and find from there a way to live with

dignity, to be and look like everyone else.' Don't try to be special or different.

AYLA: I read that after his engagement party, while she still occupied Kemal's every thought, Füsun never came to the Merhamet Apartments again. And though he grew adept at distracting himself with the happiness he found in the objects she had touched, the light had gone out of Kemal's life.

KEMAL: Forty-five minutes later, Füsun still had not come, and I was lying on the bed like a corpse, though in pain and intensely aware of it, like an animal listening helplessly to its last breath.

Beside my head was the side table on which she had left her watch so carefully the first few times we made love. For a week, I had been aware that in the ashtray now resting there was the butt of a cigarette Füsun had stubbed out. I picked it

up and rubbed the end that had once touched her lips against my cheeks, my forehead, my neck, and the recesses under my eyes, as gently and kindly as a nurse salving a wound. Distant continents appeared before my eyes, sparkling with the promise of happiness, and scenes from heaven; I remembered the tenderness my mother had shown me as a child, and the times I had gone to Teşvikiye Mosque in Fatma Hanım's arms, before pain would rush in again, inundating me.

AYLA: And Kemal began to behave like a man whose job it was to gather the refuse of his affair with Füsun. Things that had been thrown away, things that had been lost, things that were looked down on, things that had been crushed underfoot, Kemal began to collect. He felt deeply alienated from his class, and sometimes felt an affinity for the legions of Istanbul's ragpickers.

RAGPICKER: I'm quite emotional, easily hurt, so sensitive I can cry at the smallest thing. I suppose that life at night is better for people like me. I sleep during the day, no-one bothers me then, and I go out to work at night. Most people look down on me when they see me. I've noticed it, I notice it all the time. When I say they look down on you, what I mean is they look at you like you're something dirty. That's why I never go out ragpicking during the day. Night-time is the best. I always go to the same places anyway. Usually it's corporate buildings. They know me by now, so they let me in and I can roam around inside for as long as I want. No questions asked. Since people know me, I have enough work to last me through the night. I never go out during the day. I don't want to look at people during the day, I don't even want to see their faces.

AYLA: By now there was hardly a moment when Kemal wasn't thinking of Füsun. Even just walking through the streets of the neighbourhood where he had lived for most of his life caused him to suffer. For now, more than anything else, those streets reminded him of her.

KEMAL: I knew by now that if I didn't make a plan to forget her, there would be no continuing my normal daily life.

The streets or locations marked in red represent regions from which I was absolutely banned. The Şanzelize Boutique, near where Teşvikiye Avenue crosses with Valikonağı Avenue; the Merhamet Apartments, on Teşvikiye Avenue; the police station and the corner where Alaaddin had his shop – on my mental map, they were all restricted areas, marked in red.

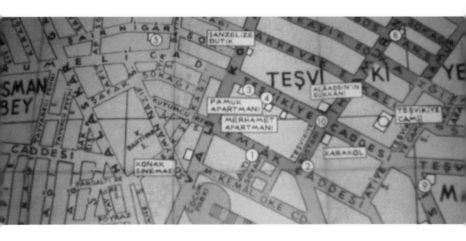

INTERVIEW, ORHAN PAMUK: The city for me is the place where the protagonist of the novel I have in my mind can walk and walk. The city bears the marks of our memories, so when we walk through its streets, we feel as if we were walking

simultaneously in the past, the present, and the future. The hero of the novel I am writing now is also always walking and selling *boza* at night. There is a quotation from Rousseau I particularly like: 'I can only meditate when I'm walking. When I stop, I cease to think; my mind only works with my legs.'

INTERVIEW, EMRE AYVAZ: You've had a bodyguard for the past few years; you go on walks together. How has this made you feel?

INTERVIEW, ORHAN PAMUK: Five months after I was awarded the Nobel Prize, and shortly after the assassination of Hrant Dink, the Turkish government began assigning bodyguards to people like me who were deemed to be in danger. Early on, when things were at their worst, I had to go around with three bodyguards. It got a little better as time went on. There is now, in 2013, greater freedom of thought in Turkey than there was in, say, 2003. I use myself as an example: I've gone down from three bodyguards to one. We're doing just fine! Having a bodyguard meant that after all those years when I had been free to wander around the city alone, there would now always be a policeman with me. As you'd expect, this rather upset me. But in time, my bodyguard and I became friends. We started going on long walks together.

KEMAL: In spite of banishing myself from the streets where I'd lived all my life and keeping far from all objects reminiscent of her, I was unable to forget Füsun. For now I'd begun to see her ghost in crowded streets and at parties.

There she was, standing before the Dolmabahçe Clock Tower, or walking through the Beşiktaş Market carrying a macramé bag like a housewife, or most surprising and unsettling, gazing down at the street from the window of a third-floor apartment in Gümüşsuyu. When she saw me in the street looking up at her, Füsun's ghost stared back at me. When I waved, she waved back. But her manner of waving sufficed to tell me that she wasn't Füsun, so I walked off in shame.

Discounting the second or two of consolation that the first sightings of these ghosts brought me, I never for long forgot that they were not Füsun but figments of my unhappy imagination. Still, I could not live without the occasional sweet feeling, and so I began to frequent those crowded places where I might see her ghost; and eventually I would mark these places, too, on my mental map of Istanbul. Those places where her ghosts had appeared most often were the ones where I was most regularly to be found. Istanbul was now a galaxy of signs that reminded me of her.

AYLA: Because he came across Füsun's ghosts when wandering slowly through the streets, staring into the distance, Kemal took to wandering slowly through the streets, always looking afar. He wanted to cry, but knowing he was guilty, he couldn't allow himself, and instead he buried his head in the sand and felt damned.

INTERVIEW, ORHAN PAMUK: If like me you've lived in the same city for sixty-two years, you will find signs pointing to your memories in every piece of the city, in its monuments, buildings, views, and trees, in its night and day, its cats and dogs, in the people on its streets, in the pavements and the squares. It's like what westerners call an 'index'. But when those buildings and those streets start to change, when they start to look different, when the old timber homes get demolished, when those late Ottoman buildings made out of wood and stone are damaged by their new occupiers, when old cinemas close down and disappear, the index to our memories begins to fade – and that is a catastrophe for each of us in its own way.

AYLA: I read that among the crowds in Taksim Square one day, Kemal saw Füsun's white shadow for almost two minutes before the illusion faded. I cannot imagine that there is a single inhabitant of this city who does not have at least one memory connected to Taksim Square and Gezi Park. In the 1930s, the old artillery barracks contained a small football stadium that hosted official matches. The famous club, Taksim Gazino, which was the centre of Istanbul's nightlife in the forties and fifties, stood on the corner of Gezi Park. And in 1977, forty-two people were killed in an outburst of provoked violence and the chaos that followed. All manner

of political parties, right-wing and left-wing, nationalists, conservatives, socialists, and social democrats, held rallies in Taksim. A square and a park that cradle the memories of millions. The only green space left in the centre of the city. Each time one of these signs is destroyed, you are faced with the distressing truth that part of your past will go with it. A new building blocks your favourite view of the Bosphorus, and there's one memory gone. Another memory is erased when a shop closes for good. A different side of you is gone when a tree is cut down. Eventually, it all disappears.

Every time a building is demolished, every time the city's roads and landscapes shift, you know that your memories too are being destroyed because no-one will be able to remember them any more. But then new people, new crowds, new stories, and new memories begin to flow into the city. And as you look towards the new skyscrapers and watch as buildings rise fast towards the sky, you notice how the city is changing with each new generation. It isn't just the city itself transforming, and your memories with it, but also the people who live there, who move along its streets and across its squares. And when you walk down those deserted streets in the middle of the night, you realise that what the city and its people remember is also changing from one generation to the next. I remember the melancholy of those empty streets in the night, the sound of memories silently fading away into nothing. Those moments when everything in the world turns inward. Those hours in which objects and streets cease to remind us of anything other than what they are. When there isn't a soul out on the streets, when the last pack of strays has retired for the night, and only the last of the street dogs is left to roam. That is when memories begin to fade away.

TAXI DRIVER: There are some streets I have trouble finding. They change the street names every few years anyway. When I first began driving a taxi, Istanbul wasn't so big, but now it keeps getting bigger. The more it grows, the more places there are that I've never heard of. New places, new streets and boulevards are born.

AYLA: It didn't take me long to accept that Istanbul was no longer the Istanbul I knew. When you spend twenty, maybe thirty years in a city, it starts to feel like a part of your own body. When we're lying in bed at night, the city streets feel like extensions of our own limbs. As we drift off to sleep, the image of the city in our minds links up with all the things we remember. And the city streets become part of the dream we are about to dream. In that moment, our memories and the sleeping city, fiction and life, all blend into one another. Were all the things written in the novel true? How much of it really happened to Füsun, and how much did the writer make up? How much of it was memory, and how much of it was fiction?

KEMAL: We have now come to the confession scene.

'Do you remember that evening in early spring, darling, when we went to Fuaye?' I began with these harmless, careful words. 'You saw that Jenny Colon bag in a shop window, and as we passed you said you liked it. We both stopped to look at it.'

My darling fiancée knew at once that this was about more than a handbag, that I was about to speak of something real and serious; as her eyes widened, I told her the story that readers will recall and visitors to the museum have known since viewing the very first object on exhibit.

I told Sibel the story in careful chronological order.

Having, of course, omitted the details of sexual bliss at the heart of my tale, I made it sound like a typical Turkish man's silly indiscretion on the eve of his marriage.

'You're a disgusting person, and it's only now I can see it,' said Sibel. Picking up an old bag of my mother's – rose-printed, and full of her loose change – Sibel hurled it at me. The loose change went flying across the floor like broken glass.

'She's a common shopgirl. She's disgusting! Are you still seeing her?'

'Of course I'm not.'

That morning, Sibel was strong and decisive in a way that shocks me even today. 'This thing you thought was love – it was just a passing obsession,' she said. 'I'll look after you. I'll rescue you from this nonsense you got mixed up in.'

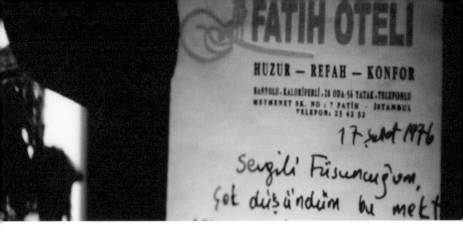

Sibel's parents had by now returned to their house in Ankara for the winter, and so the *yalı* in Anadoluhisarı was empty.

I was going to move there with her at once, abandoning all the habits that had kept me in thrall to my obsession.

From mid-November onwards, whenever we awoke on a windless night – raw from misery, or thirst, because we'd had so much to drink – we began to hear a fisherman splashing around in his rowboat, just beyond our closed shutters, moving through the still waters of the Bosphorus.

AYLA: But Kemal failed to make things work with Sibel, and when he realised that he would never be able to forget Füsun, he left the *yalı* and took refuge in the Fatih Hotel, and thirty years later, I found it standing in the same spot. Orhan Pamuk had told me how during the 1960s and 1970s, this sort of third-rate hotel had become the kind of place where bourgeois men like Kemal would come to live with their broken hearts when love, politics, or poverty made them the subject of mockery and cost them their upper-class lifestyles. We thought that Kemal's move to the hotel may have been his way of trying to overcome the difference in social class that separated him from Füsun.

INTERVIEW, EMRE AYVAZ: Love banishes Kemal from his own social class. You too have become estranged from your social class. Could you expand on this?

INTERVIEW, ORHAN PAMUK: Kemal is ostracised by the Nişantaşı bourgeoisie because of his pitiful love affair. They mock him for it. They consider it a little unseemly. I too became distanced from that same social class. I don't particularly mind, though in my case it wasn't my love for Füsun that caused me to be excluded, but my love of literature, and the political controversy in which I became embroiled. Between 2004 and 2010, I kept getting dragged into political debates. In those years, I feared for my life. I hid away and secretly came here to build the museum. The newspapers wrote that Orhan Pamuk had left Turkey and had gone to live in the United States – which suited me just fine. I would sneak out with my bodyguard and work on the museum . . . I turned into some kind of ghost.

It used to make me angry, back then, but it's in the past now and I bear no grudges. I mean it. I focused on my museum – and I wrote a love story which had little to do with politics. That worked out well. I used the money from the Nobel for the museum. There was something satisfying in tiptoeing through the backstreets of the city and slipping into the museum like a mouse. I enjoyed that quiet mood. I don't now sit around and brood over how I was treated.

KEMAL: I could not bring myself to call Sibel until the end of February. I was afraid that the dreaded talk might end in unpleasantness, anger, tears, and reproach, and hoping she might take the initiative and send back the ring with a fully justified excuse. But one day I could bear the tension no longer, so I picked up the phone and rang her; we agreed to meet for supper.

Sibel returned her engagement ring to me. Although news of her came to me from all directions, I would not see her again for thirty-one years.

AYLA: On Wednesday May 19th, 1976, at half past seven, Kemal set out for Füsun's family house in Çukurcuma. It was as if he'd forgotten all the pain he had endured since last seeing Füsun at the Hilton Hotel 339 days earlier. He was going to ask her to marry him. The car stopped in front of an old building. His heart racing, Kemal knocked on the door. Almost at once, Aunt Nesibe answered. He was climbing the stairs, and with every step he was drawing closer to Füsun. His plan had been to ignore her parents and throw his arms around her, but he could tell from the look on her face as she approached him that she didn't want him to embrace her. They shook hands. 'Oh, what lovely roses,' she said, without taking them from his hands. 'Aren't they lovely?' she said, now addressing someone else in the room. Kemal came eye to eye with the person she had indicated. 'Cousin Kemal, let me introduce you. This is my husband,

Feridun,' she said, trying to sound as if she had just recalled a detail of minor significance. 'We married five months ago,' said Füsun, raising her eyebrows as if waiting for the penny to drop.

KEMAL: After closing the door to the bathroom on the top floor, I decided that my life was no longer in my control, that my connection to Füsun had shaped it into something beyond my free will. Only by believing this could I be happy, could I indeed bear to live. On the little tray before the mirror bearing Füsun's, Aunt Nesibe's, and Uncle Tarık's toothbrushes, as well as shaving soap, brush, and razor, I saw Füsun's lipstick. I picked it up, sniffed it, and put it into my pocket.

AYLA: Kemal's first visit to the Çukurcuma house was on Saturday October 23rd, 1976. His last visit was on Sunday August 26th, 1984. He went for supper 1,593 times between those dates, an average of four times a week. Some evenings, I would see him stepping into the building to visit Füsun. He would usually bring a gift: a new hairclip for Füsun, an ornamental bowl, another bottle of cologne. Another bottle of cologne.

INTERVIEW, ORHAN PAMUK: Füsun's husband is an aspiring film director, and Füsun's dream is to star in Turkish films. Füsun and her husband both hope that Kemal, this distant relative who comes knocking at their door in the evenings, always bearing gifts, might help Füsun realise her ambition to become a film star.

Lots of films were shot in Cihangir and Çukurcuma when I was a boy, and they've started again now, after a thirty-year interval. Back in the 1960s and 1970s, whenever there was a serious family argument, whenever my parents had a fight, they would dispatch us to Cihangir. Movies were shot there because the neighbourhood was so close to the major Turkish film studios. We would stumble upon kissing scenes all the time, and there was always some security guy from the set telling us kids to 'stay away', and berating us for getting too close.

These were cheap films, and quickly made, like those black-and-white films Americans call B-movies. The actors wouldn't even bother to learn the dialogue, so a production assistant would have to call out their lines – 'I love you so much!' – shouting to make themselves heard over the noise of the generator powering the set. The actors would hurriedly

34

repeat whatever words they'd managed to catch. The whole process had us completely awestruck. *The Museum of Innocence* bears the traces of my nostalgia for that time, and my affection for Turkish film stars of that period.

AYLA: We're going into a different world, Füsun told me at the cinema one day. We could hardly wait for the curtains to part and reveal the screen. Later, I thought how those red curtains were similar to the curtains on the boxes in the museum. Füsun loved Turkish films, and Türkan Şoray's eyes.

TÜRKAN ŞORAY: He follows the woman down this road and past that mosque. We shot some scenes there. We shot over here, too. We walked over there, and behind those trees. I've been doing movies for almost fifty years. Every day, every movie I ever made has a scene shot in Istanbul. So in this city I find myself remembering, 'This is where we shot that film.' I have a memory connected to every street and every square.

AYLA: I read that from mid-June to the beginning of October 1976, Kemal, Füsun, and her husband Feridun went to see more than fifty films at the outdoor summer cinemas.

These have all gone now, but back then, the Turkish melodramas that they showed allowed us, as a community, to watch the story of our own heartbreaks unfolding on the silver screen. I wondered if it is possible that by looking at objects we might see our memories as if they were a film. The Museum of Innocence seems to have been made by those who think that this is possible, and that we carry in our own hearts the very same hope that we see emanating from the cinema crowd's gaze. Perhaps, as our soul focuses on objects, we can feel in our broken hearts that the whole world is one, and we can come to accept our sufferings.

The city was almost like a continuation of our gaze. If you were to walk out of the museum at night, you'd be forgiven for thinking the urban landscape was part of the exhibit. That shop window could easily replace one of the displays in the museum. The light over here and the darkness over there might be trickling out of Füsun's home and into the city. When Kemal left the building and went home late in the evenings, he may well have thought that the city itself was like a museum. The entire city was, perhaps, like something remembered.

'A city,' Orhan Pamuk once told me, 'will be a museum for

our memories, if we live in it long enough.' I wondered what the objects in the museum might look like at night, when it's dark and the doors have closed for the day. If no-one touched them or moved them around, if no-one ever even looked at them, they could still exist there until the end of time.

There is a story to tell every time people and objects meet. Stories exist within time. That time I bought this white handbag. That time I picked up this saltshaker. That time I dropped this earring. That time I saw this newspaper. That time I kicked this red ball. That time I wound that clock. That time I looked at this view. There is always a story to tell.

I was looking out of the window when I saw this crow. I was crying while I washed my hands in this sink. A *boza* seller walked down the street while I was listening to this radio. I thought of her while I looked at this ship. I was in love with her when I picked up this cigarette butt. Then there was another cigarette. Followed by another cigarette butt, and another. And all those cigarette butts are now a sort of calendar for the museum, a timeline of Kemal and Füsun's love story.

KEMAL: During my eight years of going to the Keskins' for supper, I was able to squirrel away 4,213 of Füsun's

cigarette butts. Each one of these had touched her rosy lips and entered her mouth, some even touching her tongue and becoming moist, as I would discover when I put my finger on the filter soon after she had stubbed the cigarette out; the stubs, reddened by her lovely lipstick, bore the unique impress of her lips at some moment whose memory was laden with anguish or bliss, making these stubs artefacts of singular intimacy.

VARIOUS VOICES: October 26th, 1976: 'Füsun, be nice to our guest.' November 15th, 1977: I don't know what they say about me behind my back. November 17th: I feel like I've been waiting forever. Be patient, Kemal. Give it time. January 30th, 1978: Ships whistle. December 1st: I stole a saltshaker off your table, like a thief. 1977: I took the rusty ladle. I took the Ankara soda bottle home.

AYLA: I wasn't aware that Kemal was holding on to everything Füsun ever touched. I only found out when I read the novel and saw the museum. Collecting objects means collecting stories, too. When you see all these objects together in one place, you end up feeling that their stories must also have happened at the same time: for in the museum, every object and every moment in time merges into one. As I looked at those objects, it was as if each display and every room was revealing the slow passage of Time itself.

INTERVIEW, ORHAN PAMUK: During my first twenty years as a writer, I used to write until four in the morning. Walking back home from my studio at night, I would always encounter packs of stray dogs. Until recently, the night-scape of Istanbul, its night hours and night-time streets, were ruled by street dogs. The French poet Nerval, the most intelligent and observant of all the modern travellers who visited Istanbul, concluded that if Istanbul's residents were so respectful towards these dogs, it was because they acted as guardians at night, and because they chewed up the city's

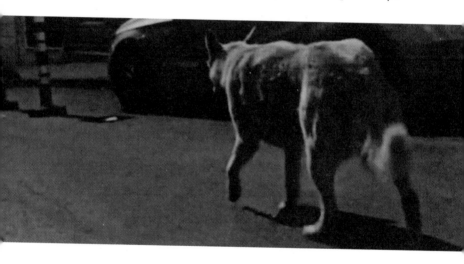

rubbish. When I was a boy, I witnessed what was, in effect, a municipal massacre of these street dogs, who were killed by the authorities in a pre-emptive measure against rabies. The story of Istanbul's westernisation is intertwined with the genocide of its dogs.

KEMAL: She took the dog from my hand and placed it on the television set. Sometimes the dogs set there brought us peace by their mere presence, much as the clock ticking on the wall did. Some looked threatening, others ugly and utterly charmless, but even these dogs made us feel as if we were sitting in a place guarded by dogs, and perhaps to feel thus protected was what brought us peace. As the neighbourhood echoed with the militants' gunfire and the outside world seemed more surreal with every passing day, the black-eared dog was the most charming of the scores of dogs that came to rest on the Keskins' television during those eight years.

On September 12th, 1980, there was another military coup.

KENAN EVREN: Certain groups have been stirring up anarchy and chaos in our country, threatening our national security and plotting a course for our nation any true patriot must abhor. I assure you that these despicable traitors will have to face the Turkish Armed Forces, and will be made to account to the Turkish people for their actions.

KEMAL: Four months after the coup we were on our way home from the Keskins' one night when, fifteen minutes before curfew, Çetin and I were stopped by soldiers checking people's identity cards.

By instinct, or by force of habit, I'd picked up the grater at the Keskins' when no-one was looking, and I'd left it sitting on the seat beside me. The grater sparkled for a moment in the glare of the bright lights of the cars waiting behind us, before I saw it disappear inside the small army truck just ahead of us. One of the soldiers came back and handed us our identity cards.

'It's all settled. You can go,' he said.

The soldier cleared the way for us. But I stepped out of the car and went over to the army truck.

'Sir, I think you still have my quince grater . . .'

'You can't keep this on your person, sir, it could be used as a weapon and cause serious injury,' said another soldier, one of higher rank. 'But fine, take it, just be sure you don't bring it out with you again.'

They didn't say anything more. I'd suffered a little heart-break, but I was glad to be reunited with the grater. I realised I was happy. These dark, empty streets that now belonged to Istanbul's dog packs, these avenues so ugly by daylight, hemmed in by concrete apartment buildings in such dreadful condition that it sapped my will just to look at them – now they looked alluringly mysterious, like poems.

AYLA: Strange times. Füsun and Feridun's marriage fell slowly and surely apart, but, over eight obsessive years, and more than 1,500 visits to Füsun's family home, through the death of his own father and a military coup, Kemal remained constant, and gradually Füsun let him back into her heart. And I remember one day Füsun casually mentioning that Cousin Kemal was giving her driving lessons. There was no better way for a young woman to be modern and independent than to know how to drive.

KEMAL: In April 1983, Füsun and I began to prepare for the drivers' licensing examination, our first tentative plans having been followed by five weeks of indecision, feigned reluctance, and silence. We both knew there would be more at stake than a licence since the intimacy between us was to be put to the test, once again in a tutelary setting.

AYLA: Füsun was very particular about the dress she wore to her driving lessons with Kemal. It was just a cheap dress we found in Beyoğlu one Saturday afternoon, but Füsun and her mother had cheerfully embellished it with Ottoman-style fastenings, and together they'd transformed it into something quite unique. Füsun used to tell me how the dress would get soaked through with her sweat during those classes. The lessons may not have taught her much about driving, but she

had begun to feel that Kemal's love for her was no longer the claim of an arrogant young man, but the love of a gentler, humbler spirit. I think it must have been during those lessons that they decided to get married. And soon, Füsun began to regard Kemal's 1956 Chevrolet as her own. And then, just like in one of those old films, after years of patient waiting, everything happened so quickly.

I read that Aunt Nesibe visited Kemal and told him that Füsun and Feridun were separating, and that Füsun wanted to meet with Kemal at the İnci Patisserie in Beyoğlu, and that the thirty-nine-year-old Kemal went to the rendezvous in Beyoğlu as happy and excited as a teenager going to see the lycée girl he had been dreaming about for months. And I read that, as Füsun took out a cigarette, Kemal leaned forward with his lighter, looking into her eyes, and, in a whisper, told her once again how much he loved her, how their bad days were over, and how, despite all the time they'd lost, a great happiness awaited them.

'I feel the same,' she said. 'We'll have a big, beautiful wedding at the Hilton, like everyone else.' She frowned gravely. 'Everything will be as it should be, down to the last detail.'

'That is how I want it, too,' Kemal said.

'There's one more thing I want. I want us all to tour Europe together, in your car. My mother will come to Paris with me. We can go to the museums, look at all the pictures. Before we marry, I also want to buy things there that I can take to our house as my trousseau.'

KEMAL: Once the car had crossed the limits of Istanbul, all the suffering I'd endured for the love of Füsun was suddenly reduced to a sweet story that could be told in one breath. After all, a love story that ends happily scarcely deserves more than a few sentences!

As we approached the Turkish border on the two-lane road, the trucks bearing down on us from the opposite direction did not even bother to dim their lights. Just past Babaeski, my eyes were drawn to the blinking purple neon sign of the Grand Semiramis Hotel; it seemed a good place to stop for the night. I asked Çetin to slow down; making a turn in front of Türk Petrol, we heard the dog's woof, woof, woof warning us off. Çetin stopped in front of the hotel, where my heart began to beat wildly, bursting with feeling, and the awareness that at this place, after nine years of longing, my dreams would come true.

AYLA: I read that, that night, in a cheap hotel on the road to Europe, both rather drunk on *rakı*, they made love for the forty-fourth and final time. And afterwards, Kemal dreamed of memories long lost and recently recovered. Images of Istanbul in old films, snowy streets, monochrome postcards passed before his eyes. He dreamed the happiness of being alive. He dreamed that dreams and memories are the same. He understood the innocence of memories. And when he woke, Füsun was gone.

And I read that he found her in the hotel garden, looking at the highway, drinking more *rakı*, and that she was half turned towards him, smoking as she waited for the sunrise, and that a black-eared dog was approaching Füsun from the direction of the gas station. And, according to the novel, as Füsun walked off along the highway, with the dog following at a distance, their final conversation went like this:

'We're all drunks now, and I would never have been like them, I assure you,' said Füsun. 'What do you mean, you're sorry!' said Füsun, angered by Kemal's response. 'You tricked me. You robbed me of my greatest treasure without benefit

of marriage, you took possession of me,' she said. 'People like you never marry what they already have. That's the kind of person you are,' she told Kemal. 'Because of you, I haven't had a chance to live my life more. I wanted to become an actress, but you and Feridun were so jealous. So afraid I might find fame and leave you that you had to keep me at home,' she said. 'What did you do with all those dogs and combs and watches and cigarettes and everything else?' she asked Kemal. 'That's a lie you just told me,' she said. 'You don't believe it yourself. That really makes me angry, how good you are at telling lies.' She said, 'On one condition. I'm driving. I want to drive now, back to the hotel.'

KEMAL: In the far distance, her friend the dog seemed to have recognised Füsun and was coming out into the middle of the road to meet the car. I was hoping he would take note of the speed and get out of the way, but he didn't.

Six or seven seconds after the crash, Füsun died of injuries sustained when the car crumpled like a tin can and the steering column pierced her chest. Her head smashed with full force against the windshield.

According to the accident report, her skull was crushed, tearing the meninges of the brain whose wonders had always surprised me, and she'd suffered a severe laceration of the neck, as well as several broken ribs and glass splinters in her forehead. All the rest of her beautiful being – her sad eyes; her miraculous lips; her large pink tongue; her velvet cheeks; her shapely shoulders; the silky skin of her throat, chest, neck, and belly; her long legs; her delicate feet, the sight of which had always made me smile; her slender honey-hued arms, with their moles and downy brown hair; the curves of her buttocks; and her soul, which had always drawn me to her – remained intact.

ORHAN PAMUK AUDIO GUIDE: Now let us take the stairs up to the attic. The attic recreates the last four chapters of the novel: the story of how, after Füsun's death, Kemal bought the house he had visited for years and converted it into a museum. When I decided to write a novel about his love for Füsun, we inevitably became friends. On many a night I sat in the attic on the chair on the right and listened to his story. Kemal would usually lie down on the bed, stare at the ceiling with his head on the bare pillow, and talk. Sometimes he'd pause, pick up the small framed photograph on his bed-side table of Füsun at the beauty pageant, and stare at it for a while. Once or twice, Kemal noticed that I was tired, and

we switched places. He sat on my chair and I lay down on the bed; suddenly I was looking at the world through his eyes, unnerved. I could easily be Kemal. I could tell my story as if it were his, and his as if it were mine. And every time I realised this, I felt that it didn't matter too much which voice was Kemal's and which was mine. Did the objects not remind us both of the very same things?

Kemal first told me his story in a single sitting. In the seven years that followed, he expanded it with details revolving around an unchanging core: his love for Füsun. I wrote the novel chapter by chapter, but he told me the story based entirely on whatever interested him at a particular moment in time – and mostly based on the objects that we could see from our vantage point in the attic. Kemal had once likened his storytelling to a spiral because, although he seemed to be drawing ever wider rings around a steady core, he could never quite break away from his starting point: love. He was then very excited to discover a similar kind of spiral pattern in Füsun's earring displayed in the first box. We later realised that the line that connected Aristotelian moments – in other words, Time – was not a straight line and that it could only be a spiral. Those who look down from the attic to the spiral of Time at the museum's entrance three floors below will see that just as the line that links moments together forms Time,

so the line that ties objects together creates a story. This, according to Kemal, is the greatest happiness a museum can bring: to see Time turning into Space.

KEMAL/ORHAN PAMUK: 'My last words in the book are these, Orhan Bey, please don't forget them.'

'I won't.'

He kissed Füsun's photograph lovingly, and placed it with care into the breast pocket of his jacket. Then he smiled at me, victorious.

'Let everyone know, I lived a very happy life.'

AYLA: So it ends as it begins: with a declaration of happiness. And while I've read the novel two or three times now, I still don't know why Füsun died. But Kemal told Orhan Pamuk that when she got into the car that night on the Edirne Road, the first thing she did was to rest her elbow on the window, just like Grace Kelly in *To Catch a Thief*. Füsun adored Grace Kelly, and Grace Kelly had recently died in a car crash on the very road she drove down in that movie. How much is memory and how much is fiction? It's been thirty years since I knew Füsun, and my own memories of her seem less real than the descriptions in *The Museum of Innocence*. But I remember she was beautiful.

INTERVIEW, ORHAN PAMUK: I don't want to exaggerate my love for the city, I don't want to go on and on about it. My relationship with this city is a bit like my relationship with my chest, my body, my hands, my arms, my family. This city is what I have been given. It has made me who I am; everything I have ever done has been built on this city. Through it, I have expressed myself.

Novel, Museum, Film . . .

As discussed in the conversation featured at the end of this book, Grant Gee planned for an interview with Orhan Pamuk to be included in the film. This interview was conducted by Pamuk's friend Emre Ayvaz, also a writer. The following pages present extracts from this long interview which did not make the cut, but which expand on the film and the museum.

Photo: Museum of Innocence archives

ÇUKURCUMA

I bought the building that houses the Museum of Innocence towards the end of 1999, four months after the earthquake that hit the Marmara region in the summer of 1999. It became the first piece of my collection: spending actual money on an empty building was a way of proving to myself that I had begun to take seriously my own idea of combining a novel with a museum. The building wasn't really vacant. Some contractor had bought it as an investment, and repurposed it as a place for his workmen to rest and recover from illness, though in rather squalid conditions. It was a sort of workers' dormitory. In those days, the neighbourhood of Çukurcuma, and the Tophane area in particular, were very poor. The building had been erected in 1897 – three years after the massive earthquake that hit Istanbul in 1894. One hundred years later – and four months after another huge earthquake – I came along and bought it. Earthquakes are a constant source of anxiety in Istanbul.

The Çukurcuma neighbourhood, now home to the Museum of Innocence, had an important role to play in the city in the 1890s. At the time, Istanbul was the de facto capital of the entire Middle East and the Balkans, and this particular part of the city was close to Bankalar Caddesi, the Avenue of the Banks, a sort of Wall Street for the Ottoman Empire. The

ethnic minorities who worked in the non-Muslim businesses of the city, the banks and the stock exchange, and who served visiting Western travellers, all lived in Çukurcuma.

By the time I bought the building, I had already decided upon certain key elements of the novel. A man falls madly in love with a woman, and when things turn out badly, he seeks, in his misery, to soothe his broken heart by collecting all of the objects connected to that woman and to the happy moments they shared. The story was there, but I had no idea yet what kind of woman she would be, her social status, her cultural background. I only knew she had to live in the kind of neighbourhood where I had decided to situate my museum, given that the museum building was going to be her family home. I had already decided that she wasn't wealthy, as the love story I had in mind turned on class differences as much as it did on sexual and gender politics. Kemal was going to be like me, an upper-middle-class man from Nişantaşı (though his family would be better off than mine), whereas the girl's family would be petit bourgeois – teachers, or tailors, perhaps. But I hadn't quite decided on that either. The kind of neighbourhood the building was in would define which class the girl and her family belonged to. For a long time I wandered around Istanbul, still undecided about Füsun's background. I wrote about these wanderings in an essay, 'Why Didn't I Become an Architect?', on how I rediscovered in this period the domestic interiors and architectural nuances of countless Istanbul neighbourhoods, the unique urban texture created by the conjunction of the city's relative poverty with its beautiful architecture, and the many ways in which the large families that have recently migrated to the city have taken ownership of venerable old homes left behind by the rich families who built them fifty, sometimes a hundred years ago. I would walk into these people's apartments in the morning to find half a dozen children watching TV and laughing amongst themselves. I would enter their homes in the guise of the inquiring buyer – always hiding my plans to build a museum. It was a happy time.

BEYOND NIŞANTAŞI

The average resident of the Nişantaşı neighbourhood would never do what Kemal did, and what I also did: beset by guilt, and disenchanted with the morals and lifestyles of the Nişantaşı set, we seized upon any reason to travel to poorer parts of the country and of the city itself. What drives Kemal apart from his social class is his heartbreak. He is derided for it. He turns inward. Füsun disappears and he searches for her in other parts of Istanbul. What do Kemal and I have in common? I too fell away from the Nişantaşı milieu where I was born and brought up. Kemal withdrew from his social class because of his broken heart; I did so because of my commitment to literature and to politics. I have no complaints, though Kemal may have been a little troubled by his lot. The 1970s Istanbul bourgeoisie I knew, and whose stories I wrote about in *The Museum of Innocence*, *Cevdet Bey and His Sons*, and *The Black Book*, did not read novels. They may have read some Balzac, in French or in translation. But they would have had no interest in reading a Turkish author. When I decided, at the age of twenty-three, that I wanted to be a writer, everyone around me – starting with my family, and with the sole exception of my father – said exactly the same thing: 'Don't bother, don't be a writer, who's going to read your novels?' Perhaps they had a point, but I didn't listen. Twenty years later, when I set out to make a museum, the same people told me: 'Don't bother; who's going to come to your museum?' Again, I didn't pay them much attention, and this time I'm not entirely sure whether I made the right decision. Still, I don't regret ignoring their advice, and finding myself telling their stories, too, in my museum.

THE EAST–WEST NOVEL

The Turkish novelistic canon includes what might be termed the East–West novel – a tradition arguably invented by Turks. In the hands of authors who believed in westernisation, this kind of novel might feature a young headscarf-wearing woman who breaks free of traditional cultural norms. Conversely, authors like Peyami Safa, busier illustrating the dangers of westernisation, might show a similar woman becoming unduly westernised and finding her virtue compromised as a result. In conveying these kinds of messages, these novelists would use different neighbourhoods of the city as code. The Fatih neighbourhood, for example, stood for the conservative past, while the Nişantaşı–Harbiye area symbolised modernity and Western lifestyles. Fatih–Harbiye is a tram line, but when it is used as the title of a novel, it also functions as a kind of plot summary. The way different neighbourhoods of Istanbul have responded to Turkey's gradual westernisation is both a helpful shorthand and an amusing diversion for writers of the city. In this sense, *The Museum of Innocence* too is an East–West novel – just like Peyami Safa's novel *Fatih-Harbiye*.

My search for the place where Füsun and her family would live, which began before I even started writing the novel, also took me to some of the city's more traditional neighbourhoods. These were often situated near Sultanahmet and Süleymaniye, places full of wandering tourists. They seemed rather shabby and poor to me at the time, though they've become wealthier now. When I walked around Fatih, I thought that someone like Kemal wouldn't really come to a place like that every night. I did a lot of exploring in that summer of 1999, both before and after the earthquake. The Fatih Hotel is a significant location in Grant's film, and it is permeated with the atmosphere that reigns in these kinds of neighbourhoods. In the end I bought a building I liked in a neighbourhood where I'd lived and roamed for years. I was sure they would never sell it. Then one day I heard it announced: 'That one's up for sale too.' I used to pass by it all the time. Every day between 1996 and 2000, I walked my

daughter to school past the same building that now houses the Museum of Innocence. I would drop her off and walk back the twenty minutes to my studio, where I would work on my novel. I would see this handsome old building on the way, though back then it was in a state of disrepair. It was a deprived neighbourhood. People would leave their rubbish outside their front doors. Still, the style, size, and location of the building seemed ideal. I thought it would be perfect as the place where my heroine Füsun would live and where a rich boy from Nişantaşı would come in his car to visit her.

Later, I entered the building for the first time.

THE CHANGING STREET

The Museum of Innocence has benefited from the gentrification of the Cihangir, Çukurcuma, and Tophane area – but it has also suffered. There is too much money now, and too much shine. The old texture has dissolved. Of course, the museum itself has also influenced the neighbourhood. Anyone who sets up a museum knows that the area around it will be somehow transformed, that the museum will draw more people in and bring wealth to the neighbourhood. I was aware these things would happen. But in parallel to this, the city as a whole has changed enormously over the past fifteen years. The novel *The Museum of Innocence* catches the city on the cusp of this change. The transformation and growing wealth of Istanbul in the past fifteen years outstrips what happened in the preceding fifty years. I spent the first fifty years of my life thinking, 'This city will never change, we will always be a poor place on the edge of Europe, among the ruins of the Ottoman Empire.' But in the fifteen years from when I bought the museum building up to 2014, Turkey has experienced a vast economic transformation. My museum came into being in the midst of all this, and the neighbourhood has since changed beyond what I could have ever predicted. Sometimes I regret this, sometimes I don't. Either way, I accept it as a part of life.

THE TRANSFORMATION OF ISTANBUL

There are so many facets to the changes in the city. When I was a boy, I used to welcome the demolition of old buildings. I was ready to embrace anything that was new, and a modern, freshly built apartment block made of concrete and glass seemed to me cleaner, more European, and inherently interesting. Like everyone else, I thought it was a good thing for those unvarnished, malodorous, musty old wooden buildings to be brought down. These attitudes started to shift in the sixties and seventies, at a time when the rich were mercilessly destroying the last few remaining wooden mansions, arranging perhaps for their caretakers or contractors to deliberately set them on fire so as to clear the way for new multi-storey blocks, and thus profit from their land. 'Look at these mercenaries,' we soon began to say, 'willing to set their own homes on fire to build apartment blocks in their

place . . .' Eventually the law changed to say that if something burned down, it had to be built back up the way it was before. But by then much of the city's glorious character had already been lost. As I write in *Istanbul*, all those wooden buildings dating back to the late Ottoman era, the soul and architectural essence of the city, were demolished, burned down, and destroyed before my eyes. Only when they realised how little was left did they finally decide to start looking after it. My whole life is the story of the demolition, the arson, the mutilation, and the transformation of Istanbul. It is also the harrowing story of the destruction of our memories, of the streets that mean something to us, of our surroundings and of sights engrained in our minds. It doesn't always have to be miserable, but it's certainly never happy. It goes beyond good and bad; when your city changes, your identity, your memory, your recollections change with it.

Let me put it simply: you're walking in Istanbul, and on your way down a hill you see a view of the Bosphorus. You happen to be in love, like Kemal. That view will forever be associated with your love and heartache. Five years later, your feelings may have changed, but you may find yourself back on that hill, and there's that view again. The moment you see it, you will recall the anguish you felt the last time you passed this place. But it can be any feeling, really: it can

be simple jealousy, or an extravagance of success, or plain joy; perhaps you'd just finished school, just sat the hardest exam, just graduated. It can be happiness that the city and its views remind you of; it can be anything.

ARISTOTLE AND TIME

In the novel and museum, I develop a simple, perhaps childish little theory of memory. We are all familiar with Aristotle's thinking on atoms. We now know that the particle we call the atom is the smallest indivisible unit that forms any object. According to Aristotle, 'moments' are like atoms: they cannot be split into smaller parts. The line that joins moments together is Time. This simple Aristotelian logic underpins the philosophy of the Museum of Innocence. Every object we see in the museum corresponds to a moment in the story of Kemal and Füsun. The straight or zigzagging line that joins those moments is the story – a story with curves, plateaus, and gentle slopes. The Museum of Innocence shows us a new way to see objects, and suggests that we look at the objects in our own lives as triggers for old memories, tools with which to retrieve the past we have lost. By arranging objects in a particular way, we can display an entire life – or even just one part of it, like Füsun and Kemal's love – in a museum.

Thus every moment comes with corresponding objects, and similarly, certain buildings in the city correlate to important times in our lives. When a building is destroyed – an iconic post office from the 1910s, perhaps, or a century-old mansion that had once belonged to this or that general, or the cinema where you saw hundreds of films in the 1950s – we don't just lose a pretty building or a potential tourist attraction, but also find that a road leading back to our memories has suddenly been barred. This is particularly true for those who live in the city. Outside visitors are less affected. They might say, 'Wouldn't it be nice if there were some older buildings left?' And we will say, 'Yes, it would be nice, but it would be even better if we could find a way back to our memories.' When an old building is demolished, when a view that means something to us is blocked, when a familiar element – even an ugly one – of the city's landscape disappears, the routes that lead back to our memories are cut off, and our sense of identity is corroded. So we embrace every part of the city – ugly or beautiful – that is old, its buildings, its views, its walls, as a way of embracing our identity. Our purpose is not to protect the city; what we're concerned with is the preservation of our memories and of our sense of self.

PROUST AND CONSCIOUS REMEMBRANCE

When the book was published and the museum opened, the nature of the novel and the museum's effect on visitors were often described as 'Proustian'. But I took this Proustian inspiration in a slightly different direction from what is usually understood by the term. The story Proust tells through the madeleine is of an unconscious remembrance. His hero eats a cake without even thinking about what he is eating, and begins to remember without even realising that he is. It is not a conscious effort. In *The Museum of Innocence*, Kemal recalls the past like someone who has read Proust. In other words, he picks up the cake in order to remember. He places Füsun's earring in a display cabinet in order to remember. He retrieves the cigarettes smoked by the girl he's just had dinner with in order to remember that moment later, and he annotates each cigarette with the specific moment it corresponds to. Proust's hero doesn't purposely set out to remember. With Proust, memories are involuntary. But for Kemal, memory is voluntary; he plans to remember. In the Museum of Innocence, even the present is something to live through so that it can be savoured in future as a memory, and memories of past happiness help to alleviate present sorrows. At home, Kemal turns to those stolen cigarette butts for solace. When he loses Füsun forever, Kemal soothes his heartbreak and grief with views of Istanbul. The landmarks and landscapes of a city don't just bring back memories, they can also amplify, or alleviate, or redirect our joy and our despair. I wanted the Museum of Innocence to demonstrate how objects can be used to mitigate life's difficulties and come to terms with our memories, with forgetting, and

with sorrow. And I wanted to show that creating a museum is in equal parts a political act – a form of cultural politics aimed at preserving our memories – and an act of private resistance, a bulwark against the vagaries of time, protecting our identity and dignity as individuals.

LIFE–HAPPINESS: THE FIRST AND LAST SENTENCES

The Museum of Innocence begins with a sentence that includes the words 'life' and 'happiness', and ends with a sentence that again includes the words 'life' and 'happiness'. The first sentence says: 'It was the happiest moment of my life, though I didn't know it,' and the last says: 'Let everyone know, I lived a very happy life.' This last sentence is also a reference to the ending of Flaubert's novel *Sentimental Education*, which contains a similar line about 'the happiest moment of our lives'.

We see and feel and experience so much when reading a novel. But novels can also subtly show us which things in life matter and which do not, what to value, which nuances to register. The ability to do this is, I think, what makes a novelist a novelist. Some writers focus on things I don't care much about, like war and money. Others instead touch on themes that are closer to my heart, and write about these as fundamental values. They are the emotions and concepts I consider fundamental in life: affection, romantic love, loneliness, fear, death, brotherhood, family, friendship. And they are the same themes that run through *The Museum of Innocence*. A novel must necessarily deal with the meaning of life and with the notion of happiness, so I deliberately started and concluded *The Museum of Innocence* with these two subjects: life and happiness. Kemal may come across as the quintessential Turkish man, self-indulgent, excessively sure of the authority conferred on him by his upper-middle-class background, and selfish. He may not seem, initially, the most sympathetic of characters. But his loyalty to Füsun and the heartache he suffers soon make us grow fond of him. Or perhaps that's just how I see it . . .

Told through Kemal's worldview, though never fully over-lapping with his perspective, *The Museum of Innocence* shows us what matters in life. The root causes of Kemal's unhappi-ness may be his exile from his friends and family, his lofty ideas about himself, his pride, his arrogance. The novel also hints at how Kemal's love affair is partly shaped by notions of pride, dominance, the rejection of male authority, a thwarted possessive impulse, and self-doubt – or at least these were some of the things I thought about when writing the book. But fundamentally, novels are made of the values they empha-sise for the world they have created, and those values were on my mind when I wrote that first sentence – 'It was the happi-est moment of my life, though I didn't know it' – and when I closed the novel with another sentence on life and happiness.

The older I get, the more I value family, happiness, and life. Perhaps I am also moving on from the experimental style and the political and East–West themes of my earlier novels. I don't think anyone will mind this shift. I changed the form of *The Museum of Innocence* while I was still writing it. When I first started, I planned to structure it as an anno-tated museum catalogue. There wouldn't be any illustrations in this catalogue, but I had in mind a list of items: first, a paragraph on Füsun's earring; second, the apple she ate one time, and a description of her expression as she ate it; and so on. All the objects were going to be listed in this way, each with its own description, and these descriptions would be arranged and organised in such a way that the novel would turn out like a carefully constructed and richly annotated museum catalogue or guidebook.

Eventually I gave up on this plan. I was already building a museum anyway. I was already being sufficiently experimental, modern, postmodern, whatever you want to call it. I thought it would be redundant to write a novel in the style of a catalogue, so at the last moment I turned it into something like a classical nineteenth-century novel.

COLLECTING OBJECTS

I started collecting for the museum while I was still writing the novel. I was lucky: Çukurcuma's junk shops were all clustered about half a kilometre from where the museum is now situated. That same area is now full of antiques stores and vintage shops, but back then it was a place where penniless students could come to buy second-hand trousers, mattresses, writing desks, and shoes. A few of those old shops persist to this day, humble, dust-ridden establishments where the difference between the buying and selling price of each article is minimal. Horse-drawn carts still roll up loaded

with used items – all sold off within minutes. All the shops in that part of Çukurcuma used to be like that twenty years ago, before the expensive antiques stores took over. I used to buy everything there. I used to walk down those same streets every day after dropping my daughter off at school and on my way to my studio to work on *Snow*, *The Museum of Innocence*, *My Name Is Red*. I knew the area well, and everything that could be bought there. Traders would call out to me: 'Mr Pamuk, we've got some new stock in, come and see.' That's how I started my collection. One thing I've noticed, in both antiques stores and junk shops: the things that end up there are only a minuscule fraction of the objects we use in our daily lives. No-one sells their old toothbrush to a second-hand store. No-one even keeps their old toothbrush. So many of the things that we use in life, and that are important to us, end up in the trash.

But there are a number of objects that fall into the category termed in the West as 'collectibles': matchboxes, lighters, bus passes, tickets to football matches, and, most importantly, anything to do with old films. Modernisation outside the Western world, in Istanbul as in all developing countries, has brought with it a mania for collectibles, but with a particular focus on cinema. I've seen this happen all over the world. Anything to do with cinema – old

movie magazines, so-called lobby cards, film reels, actor portraits, film studio ephemera, movie-star stickers from chewing-gum packets – was inherently of interest to the local collectors that began to emerge with the modernisation of the non-Western world. Füsun's dream of becoming a film star, of breaking into Yeşilçam – Turkey's answer to Hollywood and Bollywood – is a parallel for that modernisation and the accompanying passion for film memorabilia that moved the collectors who first emerged in the early years of the Turkish Republic.

Yeşilçam happens to be fairly close to the Çukurcuma area. That is a coincidence. You can't always have everything planned while writing a novel, but things do sometimes align by chance.

The quince grater from *The Museum of Innocence* is a good example of how objects can be used to tell a story.

I wanted to write about the military coup of 1980 through objects, but I couldn't seem to find a way to do it. As the people of Istanbul will often reminisce, military coups back then meant a ten o'clock curfew – though soon enough, the rules would be relaxed, and the curfew extended to eleven, and later to midnight . . . Towards ten o'clock, the police would start to limit access to key areas of the city, like Taksim, Beyoğlu, Şişli, and Karaköy. As curfew approached, people would grow increasingly anxious to get home, drive recklessly, and crash their cars – which is exactly the kind of anecdote I love to recall and write about. The police were always pulling people over to search their cars, and though nobody dared carry firearms at a time of martial law, any old thing that looked remotely sharp – knives, cutters, switchblades, and even a harmless yet unfamiliar and therefore suspicious object like a quince grater – could be considered a weapon. Thus the quince grater became a means through which I could write about the car searches and curfews at the close of the year 1980.

Using objects to explore the world in which they belong is at the heart of both novels and museums. While I was assembling my collection, I would often receive helpful suggestions from relatives and friends, or from junk dealers in Çukurcuma telling me, 'Mr Pamuk, we've got something new that might interest you, would you like to take a look?' Even after the novel was published, and as I worked to finish the museum, I continued to collect postcards, paintings, old photographs, and movie stills.

I had a 'runner', too. Runners are employed in the production of Turkish films and television serials, as well as by contemporary visual artists, for their ability to locate and retrieve particular objects. Say you are trying to recreate a post office on set, or you need a 1950s newspaper as a prop, or a thermometer of a particular shape, decorated with the picture of a mosque; the runner will find what you need. Runners will trawl through flea markets, second-hand bookshops, venerable old stores, shops in poorer neighbourhoods, the Grand Bazaar, and anywhere else that sells used items, until they find whatever it is you're looking for. Since they cannot know exactly what you have in mind, they will bring their finds to you so you can take a look before you decide whether to make the purchase. What makes runners good at their jobs is the rapport they establish with shops. Traders will let them borrow their stock: 'Take these to Mr Pamuk and let him pick something out.' Our runners at the museum would bring us things to look at every day; those moments are some of my happiest memories from the time I spent working on the museum. Each day brought an endless array of objects to consider. 'Tell Mr Pamuk to take a look at this,' shopkeepers would say. They knew what I was doing, and tailored their propositions accordingly. Some of them had even read the novel. So I would acquire objects for my collection from among their offerings. Those trinkets and pictures and photo albums made me think of people's homes, and the lives they lead in the city. Until, one day, they die, and their home, its day-to-day items, an entire life – all are gradually exposed to the world, object by object, frame by frame.

I discovered something else while I was building the Museum of Innocence. The local celebrities who used to populate the society columns had taken photographs at the parties they threw and put them in photo albums. These were the same wealthy socialites my mother and father used to tell me about when I was a child, but now those people had died, and their party albums had ended up in flea markets and from there in my hands. I used some of their photographs for the cover of the novel. Their descendants got in touch to say they'd had no idea the photographs had been lost. Some of the images I used in the museum; others I only showed to my mother. 'Do you remember this woman? She's dead now, but I've got her photo albums. They'd ended up in the flea market.' I discovered just how fragile the lives of these proud Nişantaşı middle classes, the westernised Istanbul bourgeoisie, had actually been, how ephemeral their triumphs. Working on the museum, I realised once more how readily the memory of the wealthy and upper middle classes of that period had faded away, how quickly these people whose lives we'd deemed so noteworthy had fallen into oblivion. Continuity and preservation are relatively new values among the Turkish middle classes. It is significant that although objects and photographs are the only tangible evidence of the life we have lived, old photo albums are quickly forgotten from one generation to the next. Everything, it seems, is temporary.

As described in the novel, after Füsun's death Kemal bought her house (the building that now holds the museum) from her mother, including all of the furniture and objects inside it – effectively also buying back all the things he had left there and all the gifts he had given Füsun, ready to be displayed in the museum. The additional objects given to me by Kemal, or which I found or bought from shops and gathered from acquaintances, can be considered, in Marcel Duchamp's definition, 'readymades'. But the museum also holds certain items crafted especially for the museum, and which I designed myself. Among these is the Meltem soda bottle. Turkey's first national fruit-flavoured sodas came out in the mid-1960s and early 1970s, around the time our story is set. I still remember when Coca-Cola and Pepsi-Cola first arrived in Turkey, and the day I drank my first Coke and my first Pepsi. But I liked the local sodas, too – their fruitiness and the fact that they were Turkish. I invented something similar for the novel, the Meltem soda, and enlisted some artist friends to create newspaper advertisements for it to display in the museum. These advertisements are not readymades, but fresh creations made purposely to look as if they were bought from vintage shops. So the collection is composed of objects that I've gathered or taken from Kemal, and objects that we commissioned specifically for the museum because we couldn't find anything already in existence that

Photo: Museum of Innocence archives

matched the events narrated in the novel. There are also items that lie somewhere in-between. They may have served one purpose back in the day, but we've used them in a different context – or we've modified them a little to align more closely with how they appear in the novel itself . . .

I've always liked to boast about a comment we once had from a visitor: 'I went to the Museum of Innocence and came out hungry!' The museum displays the kinds of meals that Istanbul's middle-class families – whose lives are the subject of the novel and the museum itself – used to eat back in the sixties, seventies, and eighties. We can't keep actual food on display, of course. Instead, we've sculpted near-perfect replicas of those dishes, painted to look as real as possible, and which may indeed trigger hunger pangs in visitors with particularly healthy appetites. Food is rarely displayed in most museums, and even when it is, it is considered a lesser component within the wider collection. But in our museum, you can find a photograph next to an expensive ashtray or an Ottoman crystal artefact, next to an ordinary plate of food, next to another photograph . . . Like a Dutch still-life painting which brings together in one frame all kinds of objects from our daily lives, plain or precious, ordinary or significant, simple or allegorical, inviting us to observe and interpret life through these objects and draw from them some kind of new meaning, the Museum of Innocence shows us that life will surround us with a vast and varied range of objects, from morsels of food to postcards of beautiful views, from valuable items to forgotten scraps, from discarded newspapers to identity cards, and leads us to consider what we might learn from this fact.

I'm not convinced that conserving the past is only about preserving so-called 'collectibles'. Smells, sounds, tactile experiences can and should also be preserved. The Museum of Innocence is, among other things, an aural museum. We sought out and recorded the noises of the city, its secret voice, and the sound of the horns of its ferries, for which the museum is now a repository. You will hear three types of sounds in the Museum of Innocence. The first kind is

activated automatically as you approach certain display cabinets, sounds like the 'hooooot' of the ferry horn, so familiar to all those who live in Istanbul, and which helps to convey the general mood of the city. Secondly, though you may not even realise that you are hearing these sounds, other visitors will perceive them as distant and intermittent notes. Finally, there is the faraway sound of a foghorn or a freight ship's whistle that can be heard throughout the entire museum, but which plays only once every forty-five minutes, so that in order to hear it twice, you would have to spend at least two hours in there. At one point we had plans to recreate smells, too, but have yet to put those into practice.

NOVEL–MUSEUM

I started thinking in the early 1990s about a linked novel and museum. I mulled it over for a few years until I grew convinced it would be impossible. But then one day I put down the cash and bought the building. Now I had no choice but to forge ahead. All the people who had told me twenty years ago, 'Don't bother with novels, Orhan, go and be an architect or an engineer, get a real job,' were now saying, 'Orhan, you've somehow made it as a novelist, but a museum, well, that's too much; don't do it.' So I decided not to tell anyone what I was doing. I began to collect objects from shops in Çukurcuma and from relatives, never revealing what they were really for and saying instead, 'I just really like this stuff, I'm a bit obsessed' – like Kemal. As my collection grew, I studied the items I had gathered and related them to Füsun's story, to Kemal's story, to the love that brought them together, and to the Istanbul landscapes that formed the background to their affair. The Museum of Innocence doesn't just display objects from life in Istanbul between 1950 and 2000, but also the landscapes that its citizens saw, the films, postcards, and newspapers of that era, poignant mementoes of the old Istanbul, and anything my collaborators and I were able to find that could illustrate Füsun and Kemal's romance.

When I first started writing the novel and assembling objects, I didn't dwell too much on how exactly I would display things in the museum. There was enough to think about already, and I preferred to focus on the novel for the time being, and set the collection aside until I was ready. I finished the book and published it in 2008. But I was under some political pressure in those years, and besides, I didn't even have the kind of money you might need to build a museum, so until the Nobel Prize I wasn't quite sure what to do. I had begun to think that the museum would never be anything more than a dream, that the building I'd bought would remain as it was, with the objects I'd gathered all stored in my house, that I'd forget everything and start working on a new novel entirely, and simply move on. But with the Nobel

Prize, and with the increasing sales of my books, the money I needed fell into my lap.

After the novel came out in 2008, I made up my mind to complete the museum. I'd expected to be done within six months, but it took four years to finish – despite the vast collection I'd already gathered. Of course, it only took so long because I wanted to make the display boxes look beautiful. I couldn't bear to just lay them out on a table, stick a few labels on, and leave it at that, as if it were some ordinary state museum.

I am at heart a failed painter, a fact which undoubtedly also played its part. The dormant painter inside me was revived by the sight of all these objects, and wanted to turn the vitrines in which they would be displayed into works of art. I wanted to make a beautiful exhibit of each cabinet; in other words, the painter inside me wanted to use these objects to make art. That's why it all took longer than predicted. Here we are five years later, having this conversation in 2014, and I have yet to publish my new novel. It's not all Mevlut's fault; it is also because I devoted two and a half years of my life to the museum.

ISTANBUL IN OLD FILMS

Only as I got older did I learn to pay attention to what was going on in the background of Yeşilçam movies set in 1960s Cihangir. Back then, like every other boy my age, my attention was solely on Türkan Şoray and Müjde Ar's faces in the foreground. I've watched them all again since then to focus expressly on the black-and-white Istanbul landscapes in the background, which have now become an integral part of my enjoyment of the films, as much as the formidable presence of Türkan Şoray, Müjde Ar, or Hülya Koçyiğit in the foreground. Those cinematic landscapes have become inseparable in my mind from the kissing scenes to which they provide the backdrop, much as Istanbul forms an integral part of Füsun and Kemal's love story. And the kisses, the fistfights and car chases filmed over those old and crumbling cityscapes have become fundamental components of the image of Istanbul in my mind.

Nowadays, if you're yearning for a glimpse of the Istanbul of your childhood, there is a film channel on TV that can help. Every now and then a friend will call me: 'Orhan, quick, they're showing that scene!'; 'See how different that street looked; look what that place used to be like before it all changed . . .' We've spent our whole lives feeling either shocked or thrilled by the transformation of Istanbul. 'They're knocking the old buildings down, we're going to be modern!' we would rejoice when we were children. 'They're

knocking the old buildings down, we're losing our culture!'
we now protest.

THE HILTON HOTEL IN ISTANBUL

The first thing that the Hilton Hotel showed us was that westernisation and economic growth in Turkey were processes
pioneered by the wealthy, and enabled by bureaucrats and
the upper classes. In my boyhood, there was a widespread
notion – rather narrow and irksome – that leading a westernised lifestyle meant travelling to Europe and back for
glorified shopping trips to Paris or London. The Hilton Hotel
is to me a symbol of that shift in consumption habits that
can be termed 'wardrobe westernisation'. Now the glitter and
charm of those days have been supplanted by the effects of
mass tourism. The Hilton's old pomp has faded.

I have another memory associated with the Hilton. It was
after the military coup of 1980, and incidents of horrific tor-
ture, oppression, and custodial death had reached their peak.
A PEN delegation consisting of Arthur Miller and Harold
Pinter had come to Turkey, and I was to act as their guide.
Harold Pinter's suitcase never arrived, and we were all quite
paranoid, worried that we were being followed. Everybody
became very cautious.

Miller and Pinter were staying at the Hilton, so we would
meet up there. We knew we were being followed, though we
weren't doing anything illegal. We would sit in the hotel and
talk about politics, while laughing about our slightly preten-
tious, not quite Turkish surroundings.

The house in Nişantaşı where I lived while I wrote *My
Name Is Red* faced the Hilton. The Hilton is like a wall that

divides Nişantaşı from Taksim. The residents of Nişantaşı like to go shopping in Taksim and Beyoğlu. On the way, they'll have a slice of cake at the Hilton, which lies in-between.

When the Hilton first opened in the 1950s, it became the favoured haunt of the Istanbul bourgeoisie. They used to move in small circles back then. But things have changed, and the Hilton is no longer the exclusive spot where the city's upper middle classes come to socialise.

ISTANBUL AND WALKING

When I was a child, people were fascinated with cars – or 'automobiles', as they were known back then. Not everyone had an 'automobile'. People used to walk, or take public buses. I enjoy walking in the city, and so do the heroes of my novels. The best thing about modern cities is the way they bombard you with pictures, images, dreams, objects, billboards. I love that feeling. When he walks around the city, Kemal is looking for Füsun, but also reflecting on the nature of his love, and trying to relieve his anguish – as he also hopes to do through Füsun's belongings and her discarded cigarette butts.

In a way, Istanbul 'made' me. I've spent my whole life in this city. Istanbul has determined the course of my life, defined me, and raised me. In 2006, I accepted a job offer from Columbia University, which meant that every year, I spent four months away from Istanbul to teach a semester there. Political pressures certainly played a role in my decision to take the job. The change served me well. It allowed me to evaluate certain aspects of the museum and the novel from an external vantage point. Writing about a city when you're somewhere else gilds and sweetens your view of it.

The Museum of Innocence is in parts a novel written by someone who has been separated from a city but loves it all the more for that.

When I first began to write, I didn't really think, 'I want to be a writer of Istanbul.' What I thought instead was, 'I want to be a good writer.' A good writer needs stories about people to investigate their humanity. Like all writers, I was writing about people I knew, my people, the people I'd met in

Istanbul. From the late 1990s onwards, when my books began to be translated into foreign languages, I realised that writing about the people I encountered in the city had made me into a writer of Istanbul. Before then, it had been an unconscious inclination: I had always written about Istanbul, but it had never occurred to me that this was what I was doing. Borges said that there are no camels in the Qur'an. That's not quite true, but what Borges meant is that when you become too conscious of something about your identity, and what other nations think of its signs and symbols, that self-awareness can hinder your sense of authenticity. During the first half of my life as a writer, I never realised that I belonged to Istanbul. But in the second half, as I worked on the Museum of Innocence, I understood that I belong to this place, and I carry that understanding with me as I write today. This shifting awareness has also changed the way I look at the city.

In my first twenty years as a writer, before my daughter was born, I would write until four in the morning, then go to sleep and wake up at noon. I used to walk back home from my studio in the middle of the night. At that hour, the city is deserted, save for packs of street dogs. It's as if the city were abandoned. In the 1970s and 1980s, it wasn't particularly safe, either. In my mind, the lone mysterious figure walking through the city streets at night became connected, in the 1970s, with violent street clashes between left- and right-wing militants and people putting up posters and writing slogans on walls, and in the 1980s with the curfews that were imposed after the military coup. You follow the shadow of a dog on a wall over here, you see beggars or stray cats and dogs rummaging through a bin over there, you come across people going to work or returning from their night shifts, and slowly the small textile workshops behind Nişantaşı start to open . . . In the city, in Istanbul, life never stops. Even at the quietest hour – even at four thirty in the morning – you will hear the distant put-putting of a little boat on the Bosphorus, the whistle of a ferry, the clang of an engine, the last drunk out on the streets, or the first few people to wake up for work . . . My ears and my mind are attuned to each of these sounds, their shifts and motions, the way they move the air, and so too to the padded footsteps of dogs and stray cats. As I observe all this, I imagine a man – a man who's been drinking, perhaps, but maybe he is just a little tired, or irritated, or melancholy – walking in the darkness or the twilight of the city, through courtyards and secret alleys, and I imagine putting that man's inner world at the centre of a novel. Maybe that man is me; maybe we are alike. It would be interesting to look at the world through his eyes. This man who is on his way home at four in the morning, just like me . . . where is he coming from? Where is he going? There is a satisfaction in puzzling over this kind of question, and it usually means I have begun to envision that man as part of a story, a dream, a novel I might write someday. If I have started to imagine the story of a man walking alone in the middle of the night down an eerie and dangerous street, I have also started to imagine a new novel.

I still go for walks in Istanbul. One of the joys of having a bodyguard is that you can walk anywhere, to dangerous streets, through threatening neighbourhoods where you would not go by yourself at night, and discover remote, gloomy places you wouldn't otherwise be able to visit. I love these long walks; after all, I'm a novelist. Thanks to my bodyguard, I can see new and distant parts of the city I wouldn't have the courage to explore alone. Or when I walk past the inner courtyard of a building I've never seen before, I might think to myself, 'So what if it's private property, I can still go in, I've got my bodyguard with me.' We've developed an understanding now. Sometimes I'll walk ahead and he'll fall back – fifty metres, five metres, thirty metres – to a distance determined by our surroundings. There are some places where I'd be embarrassed to be seen with a bodyguard, so I'll ask him to 'please hang back for a while'; showing up with a bodyguard to the neighbourhood I lived in for years would feel like something to be ashamed of, a kind of failure. But sometimes we'll walk side by side and talk. I suppose we've become friends. I'll tell him about the way the city used to be, just as I would tell my readers. 'They knocked that building down,' I'll say, 'and they built this in its place, and these streets used to look completely different...' We've

often gone about the city like a pair of tourists. The bodyguard is essential for any night-time trips to more isolated and unfamiliar neighbourhoods. In fact, his presence has encouraged me to go on even more walks and explore more places. I have learned to enjoy having a bodyguard behind me as I discover the city's hidden nooks, its strange chemistry, its inner silences and enchantments.

The Russian literary critic Viktor Shklovsky had a theory that what we call a story is actually a line that joins the moments, scenes, and subjects we wish to describe. Just like the line that, according to Aristotle, joins up moments to form Time. The novel too is a line that joins up moments into a story. When I walk in the city I see reminders of my past in the landscapes, objects, buildings, shop windows, trees, walls, and images around me, each loaded with its own particular memories. These visions run through my mind like scenes from a novel. Walking briskly through the city, in the daytime or at night, I feel sometimes as if I were wandering around inside the first draft of a novel I've written myself.

On days when I feel emboldened to experience something different, I head for Istanbul's new districts, telling myself, 'This road will surely lead me in the right direction.' Or we might make plans with friends – 'Let's meet in Taksim Square,' or 'See you at the pier' – and instead of going the same old way, I'll pick a different street I've never used before. I guess everyone does that every now and then. But sometimes all I want is to feel safe, so I'll choose the route I've taken a hundred times before, perfectly happy to take it a hundred and one times if necessary. It's the same with Tolstoy or Dostoevsky. There are certain scenes from my favourite novels of theirs that I've probably read a hundred times and would happily read again. They are a source of security and strength. Being a novelist is about seeking out what feels unfamiliar and uncomfortable, finding new topics, and constantly challenging yourself to evolve. But the urge to write is also connected to a yearning for home, for the feeling that you are treading on solid ground, in the place which forms the core of your existence.

ART-MELANCHOLY

My youthful ambition to become a painter was a defining moment in my life. I still paint. I'm a relatively visual writer. I tell my stories through images, and envision them at first as scenes and tableaux. A painting is the visual manifestation of a moment: the passage of time does not apply. Between the ages of fourteen and eighteen, I took photographs out on the streets of Istanbul so I could later paint what I saw. I have published a selection of these photographs in my book *Istanbul*. Every time I went out into the city to take these preparatory photographs, I would feel myself becoming imbued with a specific emotion. I decided that this emotion should lie at the heart of my book. I am talking, of course, of *hüzün*, the 'Turkish melancholy' described in that book. As Baudelaire and his nineteenth-century colleagues discovered and described at length, the way we are affected by the representation of a landscape depends on the emotions we associate with that landscape.

In *Istanbul*, I sought to deconstruct the sense of melancholy the city emanated during my youth. I have always tried, in my books, in the photographs I've taken, and the paintings I've made, to identify and capture the kinds of scenes that make us feel melancholy. My work as a writer and an artist is founded on a commitment to finding the sources of the emotions the city makes us feel, and to immortalise these through writing, painting, and photography.

There is a social dimension to our so-called Turkish melancholy, relating to an awareness of our distance from Europe while finding its economic and cultural prosperity to be lying just beyond our reach. The sense of an ongoing failure to match our neighbours' achievements leads to a kind of withdrawal, a bitterness and resentment towards life. But in *The Anatomy of Melancholy*, Robert Burton argues that melancholy can be a source of pride, an idiosyncrasy, an inspiration for art and nonconformity. The *hüzün* I describe in *Istanbul*, though, is a force that engenders a sense of community, a feeling of resignation, of looking inward, and not venturing and manoeuvring for success. This sentiment forges a collective spirit and enables us to share the same meals, the same emotions, the same joys and woes. Rather than the unique melancholy felt by the individual, what I describe in *Istanbul* is the *hüzün* we all experience.

In *The Museum of Innocence* and other books, I have tried to connect the city's many neighbourhoods through their communal feeling of melancholy. *The Museum of Innocence* and *Istanbul* in particular have much in common; these two books – both of which I published recently, and which are especially connected to Istanbul – seek in the city a mirror for the characters' emotions.

I had hoped to display some of Füsun's own paintings in the Museum of Innocence. I wished I could become Füsun and paint them myself. It hasn't happened yet, but that doesn't mean it won't some day. The Museum of Innocence opened in 2012. I will be expanding it with new pictures, new cabinets and displays until the day I die. Right now, I'm working on Füsun's bird sketches. Like her, I too wanted to be a painter. I wrote in *Istanbul* of how, from when I was seven up until I turned twenty-two, my family encouraged me to become an engineer, while the engineers in my extended family advocated for me to become a painter. So I grew up thinking that was what I would do. Then one day, when I was twenty-two, a screw came loose in my head and I declared, 'Never mind painting,

I am going to be a novelist.' I forgot – or tried to forget – about painting. Now, thirty years later, the hidden painter inside me has come back to life and created the Museum of Innocence.

I still paint now, and feel that I have a talent for both painting and literature – 'sister arts', as they were once known. I am much happier and more fully myself when painting, and if I've had a glass of wine beforehand, it can almost feel as if my hand were drawing of its own accord while I watch and wonder at its motion. My mind works a lot harder when I am writing novels, and I am less happy. I have to put more effort into it. But I am more satisfied with the results. Sometimes I think that if I exercised my mind more while painting, and wrote novels more light-heartedly, I'd be both a better writer and a better painter. Painting and literature seem to me essential elements of our basic humanity. I understand why artists paint, and often wish I could be in their place. Now that I'm a famous writer, I'll take any opportunity to be introduced to the artists I admire. I visit their studios, talk to them, try to enjoy their daily lives and humanity. I see in each of them the person I secretly wish I could be.

DOGS AND THE CITY

In the years between 1973 and 1996, I was a nocturnal writer, and on my way home at night I would always encounter packs of stray dogs. *My Name Is Red* opens with a monologue from a street dog in Istanbul in the 1590s. Istanbul at night used to be dominated by dogs. Ottoman sultans and pashas who were particularly eager to imitate the West would regularly embark on the mass slaughter of these dogs. Doctors and public health officers would provide some convenient scientific justification for these culls. During the day these dogs would ambush pedestrians, soil the streets, and roam around in total freedom, in a manner considered unbefitting of the European lifestyle. So the dogs would periodically get picked off the streets and exiled to the remote island of Hayırsızada, in the Sea of Marmara. In those days it was a common occurrence for strays to be rounded up thus and dumped onto uninhabited islands, or eliminated in genocidal massacres. Deprived of their strays, the public would react by rallying together to petition the sultan: 'We want our dogs back.' The sultan would change his mind, or a new government, less ambitious about its westernisation project, might meanwhile come to power, and eventually the hapless dogs would be allowed to return. But if you ask me, the true existential threat to these dogs has emerged in the last twenty-five years, and the specimens we see now will be the last of their kind. The problem is that garbage containers have been modernised. In the past, dogs would knock bins over and survive on the rubbish that spilled out. That was why I would always see stray dogs when I wrote at night. Their lives revolved around knocking over trash cans. But now bins have lids that won't open, and come in big black containers made of metal or plastic, the final phase in the annihilation of these dogs. I love looking at the city through

these dogs' eyes, though I do have some distressing child-hood memories about them. More recently, in the 1990s, I was cornered by a pack of strays and bitten, and had to get a rabies shot at the infectious diseases hospital in Sultanahmet. Nevertheless, I have a cordial rapport with street dogs. Not that you must have a good relationship with someone in order to write about them effectively. I'm still scared of them. Perhaps it's this fear that compels me to write about them.

Like the hero of *A Strangeness in My Mind*, the novel I am finishing now, I always tell myself when I come across these dogs that there is nothing to be afraid of. But I fear them anyway, I find myself thinking about them, and as I do I gradually begin to identify with them.

WRITING BY HAND

Sometimes I think I must be the last person left who still writes by hand. But I know there are other writers like me who still do that. When I was younger, I thought typewriters were for journalists, and as I was a writer, I needn't bother. By the time computers appeared, I'd been writing for a long time, and I didn't want to change my habits. I write very slowly. I can toil for a day and come away with half a page or a page at most. I didn't want to spend all day staring at a computer as if it were a miniature aquarium. The first computer screens made my eyes water. Maybe that's why I never managed to make the switch. But I'm all right with that.

I write by hand, patiently, my eyes always on the page. I take pleasure in watching the pen advance over the page like a paintbrush, in the smell of ink and paper, in the sight of the scattered sheets, erasers, and scraps of paper around me.

I write a little, and then I go back over it to make corrections. When the page becomes too messy, I tear it off and write it out again, and again, and again. Writing, for me, is about rewriting, patience, endless deliberation over what to say next, and conserving what I've already written. That's the work ethic I've adopted.

In the Ottoman era, poets were respected figures. Not every Ottoman sultan was a poet, but about a third of them thought about producing a collection of poetry, perhaps written with the help of well-paid master poets of the time. There was an abundance of poets in the upper echelons of Ottoman society, among ministers, grand viziers, and religious scholars. Putting together a *divan*, a collection of poetry, signalled a certain level of education, refinement, and cultural elevation. That explains why so many Ottoman sultans wrote poetry regardless of whether they had any talent for it: to demonstrate that they had mastered the poetic conventions of their time. They would write poetry collections to prove they were able to write something meaningful while still respecting those conventions, and in doing so would bolster their intellectual credentials. No wonder being a poet in Ottoman times was a source of distinction. To this day, being a novelist, a storyteller, is not deemed as prestigious an occupation. When I first started writing, novelists in Turkey were perceived as being 'basically like clerks who sit and write all day'. Poets, on the other hand, were seen as venerable figures with important things to say, who received their words straight from God. Those who wrote novels were not so gifted, and had to labour instead like patient ants, marathon runners on a never-ending course. Writing novels was also seen as a less innovative occupation. This, together with the familiarisation of the classic nineteenth-century novel, and a disdain for the more unconventional and experimental, modern and postmodern kind of writing I favoured, has resulted in fiction writers being regarded as lesser beings compared to poets. That suits me. When I first started writing, even I saw myself as a kind of clerk, and my ambition was to take the things I saw around me and place them in orderly fashion within the framework of a longer narrative. Sure, I wanted to experiment. But I've always eschewed the exalted roles, the vigorous intellectual stances our poets have traditionally embraced.

CIGARETTES AND SUGGESTIVE HAND GESTURES

I smoked a lot of cigarettes during my first twenty years as a novelist. I rapidly burned through my God-given quota, and then gave up. I've struggled against cigarettes all my life. Like giving up smoking, writing is a test of willpower. Everything seems to tempt you away from your desk: meeting up with friends, a party at your neighbours', a film at the cinema, and the latest televised scandal. The book you are writing might be unhelpfully complicated. But you must will yourself to keep writing, just as you would to give up smoking. I've been writing all my life; it's been more than forty years now. And I've always known that my greatest strengths are discipline, perseverance, and resolve.

We smoke 'like Turks'. There are endless implications to how we talk and gesticulate while we smoke, enough to keep any anthropologist busy. 'Here, have a cigarette,' we'll say as an overture of friendship, or as the starting point of any communication among Turkish men. If they hesitate to take the proffered cigarette, we'll quickly produce a lighter – both to show it off, and to demonstrate how obliging we are as a sign of our deepening friendship. Then there is the manner in which we stub out the cigarette: with one of Füsun's irritable gestures, or flicking it away just so, like a proper existentialist might, or carelessly tossing it to the floor. A cigarette can be crushed furiously underfoot. There are cigarettes for the wealthy, and cigarettes for the poor: the local Birinci brand, and smuggled American cigarettes of the seventies and eighties . . . In the years when *The Museum of Innocence* is set, only Turkish cigarette brands could legally be sold in Istanbul. Other brands were only available through illicit channels. This is something I touch upon in the novel. Carrying Marlboros became a marker of prestige, proof that one had the means to find and acquire them. Smoking for me used to be at once a vice and an anthropological investigation. An accomplished novelist must master the act of lighting a cigarette and the range of significant meanings it can convey before setting out to describe these to the reader. In the Museum of Innocence, every cigarette Füsun smokes, every cigarette she lights, is paired with an expression, a movement, a gesture – all recreated in appositely recorded videos – that reveals something about the heroine's state of mind in that moment. In the museum, we show Füsun smoking. Kemal collected more than 4,200 cigarette butts she discarded, gave them all to me, and told me how each one should be captioned. In the summer of 2011, I did what was expected of me: I wrote underneath each cigarette a few words that would reflect Füsun's various moods as witnessed and relayed to me by Kemal, and in keeping with the spirit of the novel.

We've discussed how every object in the Museum of Innocence corresponds to a particular moment. Every cigarette stub Kemal retrieved and took away from the ashtray or the table where Füsun had left it was in some way emblematic of Füsun's relationship with Kemal, or of Füsun's mood in that moment, or of the things she said and did while she smoked. Here's how Füsun felt while she smoked this cigarette; here is what was happening in that moment. So in the context of our Aristotelian conception of time, cigarette butts are displayed in the museum as a sign of that moment.

When you stand back and look at the cigarettes on display, you might think, 'These all look the same to me.' But if Kemal and Füsun could visit the museum, they would notice all their nuances and various accompanying feelings. Each of those cigarettes is a new turn, a new phrase, a new paragraph in a story whose complexion seems to endlessly shift, and in doing so to keep its readers' interest alive.

ON FÜSUN

If Füsun were alive today, I would like to think of her as a beautiful, slightly preoccupied woman, working in an office somewhere, with ambitions to rise through the ranks of the company, bold but wary of predatory men, and striving ultimately for happiness. Füsun's distressing story is in some ways the story of all Turkish women. Men crush women under the force of their love. They use their love to justify their oppressive demands. 'I love you too much to let you leave the house,' they'll say; always 'I love you too much . . .' They refuse to let women develop their own identities. And it doesn't just happen in Turkey. Over in this half of the world, men who wield any sort of authority over the women they love will try to force them into certain roles. Füsun hopes to exploit the roles these men offer her. She tries to get what she wants by way of what men want; unfortunately, what she wants is to become a Yeşilçam film star. Not by accident, her husband is a film director. I've thought a lot about Füsun. But when I've tried to picture her, or to put myself in her place, I've found my gaze and my insight limited by my gender. This is the moral dilemma that makes writing novels such an attractive proposition. A novel isn't just a vehicle through which to write about yourself. It also requires you to write about those who are not like you, who are, for whatever

reason, a little different – in class, gender, culture, or religion. The talent of any novelist is based on their will and the ability to write their own story as if it were someone else's, and someone else's story as if it were theirs.

ART–LITERATURE: AM I KEMAL?

I dreamed of becoming a painter before deciding to become a writer, so I have always been intrigued by the correspondence between a world created through words and a world created through paintings and objects. A work of literature operates through time. Stories have a beginning and an end; between them runs time. But a painting deals with space. It portrays a moment. It covers a scene. This similarity between the two mechanisms – how the work of art exists in space and the work of literature exists in time – must be what the German philosopher Heidegger meant when he referred to the 'thingness of artworks'. Here I am, sitting alone, writing a novel, a work of the imagination. Then I start to gather real objects, and envision a museum for the novel. Then, I actually purchase a building and start setting up the museum. I work diligently to turn it into something worthwhile. Finally, that museum I had imagined becomes reality. Soon there are street signs cropping up around the neighbourhood, pointing in the direction of my museum. Even I am still taken aback every time I see one. Even I forget sometimes that it is my own creation to which they point, when, walking on the street or sitting in a taxi, thinking distractedly about one thing or another, I suddenly look up and see a sign that says this way to the Museum of Innocence.

Each of these signs reminds me that what I had imagined has become reality. I'm not too surprised that it has: I know that art and literature are inexorably linked, that the Museum of Innocence is rather like a novel, and that my novels are themselves like museums. Still, if you were to ask me, 'When you started writing your first novel at the age of twenty-three, did you ever imagine that it would lead to a museum, more books, libraries, translations into sixty languages, and all the rest that's happened?', I would tell you no, I could never have imagined it. I deal with it sometimes by pretending it's all happening to someone else.

Some of the things I have written about love have later happened to me in real life. After *The Museum of Innocence* was published, I had a lot of inquisitive readers, particularly women, wondering about Kemal's obsessive, feverish love for Füsun. So many times I have been asked, 'Orhan Bey, are you Kemal?' Of course there are certain aspects of my own experience which resurface in the stories of those characters from my novels who are most like me. But it is a peculiarity of the art of the novel that even if you tell readers of a love story like Kemal's that 'it's a novel, it's all fiction', they won't want to believe you. They will think instead, 'He would never have been able to describe it so well if he hadn't been through the same thing himself.' A reader's refusal to believe that you've never experienced first-hand the things you've written about is a compliment to your literary capabilities, your style, the force of your book. The best thing to do is to accept the compliment and tell them with a knowing wink, 'Yes, I am Kemal.'

VISITING THE MUSEUM

Visiting the museum is not a prerequisite for enjoying the novel. The novel can stand alone. And I'm pleased to say that reading the novel is not essential to enjoying the museum. In fact, even people who've read the novel before coming to the museum start to behave, fifteen minutes into their visit, as if they hadn't read it at all.

Visitors to the museum can be placed into two groups: those who've read the novel, and those who haven't. The first few display cabinets correspond to the initial chapters of the novel, so at the very start of their visit, those who've read the book find themselves thinking back to it and gleefully matching each object to its twin in the novel.

For these visitors there is something understandably satisfying in studying the displays and recognising objects described in the pages they remember reading, or which they may be perusing again from their copy of the book (or from one of the museum's copies, attached to the displays). This usually goes on for the first ten to fifteen minutes of their visit.

But soon enough they start to behave exactly like the visitors who haven't read the book. They stop seeing the museum as if its purpose were to follow a particular story.

Instead they begin to understand it as the representation of an emotion. Of course, the Museum of Innocence functions as an enactment of the plot of *The Museum of Innocence*, but more than that, it is the embodiment of a feeling, a state of mind, a place created to convey the mood and atmosphere of the novel, the story of a wretched love affair, and the soul, the texture of a provincial city at the margins of Europe in the fifties and sixties. Visitors who recognise this atmosphere may well find themselves drawn back to the story. But I know from my own observations, and from the way visitors behave, that the museum conveys primarily an essence, a mood, an atmosphere. It is an atmosphere built on a love story, on feeling provincial, on belonging to a poor outpost on the edge of Europe. The love story, the museum, the novel all hinge on the hardships experienced by a lower middle class with no way up, and on the futility and precariousness of their lives.

Your perspective on the museum will vary depending on whether you read the novel before your visit, after your visit, or not at all. But your fundamental response to what you see will not differ so greatly. If you've read the novel, the museum will give you access to the intimate details of its characters' lives. You will see how a lighter, a driver's licence, or a newspaper clipping can illuminate a life, and at the same time the museum will show you that driver's licence or that newspaper in a different light. You might perceive a different sort of energy from what you observe. But even if you haven't read the novel, you will still be able to savour the mood invoked by those same objects. Of course, I'm glad if people read the novel before or after visiting the museum. But I'm sure that those who come without having read the book can enjoy the museum as much as those who have.

After *The Museum of Innocence*, I wrote a manifesto for museums. My aim was to use the manifesto form to explain in simple terms what I was trying to achieve in my museum. The word 'manifesto' tends to evoke images of angry, impassioned youths with powerful ideas. I am no longer an angry young man, but I do love museums. The manifesto of the Museum of Innocence is against large, institutional, state-sponsored museums that tell the history of a nation and its people. Of course, I love and enjoy those kinds of museums, too. But what I'm trying to express in my manifesto is this: in the modern era, humanity has progressed from the enjoyment of epic sagas to the pleasures of the novel. Today, the equivalents of those sagas are major institutions like the Louvre and the British Museum. National museums are concerned with nation states, the lives of kings, and ancient history. We've moved on from sagas to novels which tell the stories of individual human beings, but we still haven't managed to make that transformation when it comes to museums. Unfortunately, museums today – particularly in non-Western countries – still operate as epics, more concerned with flag-waving and acting as repositories of the signs and symbols of national identity. I think that museums should concentrate on the stories of individuals, and be founded upon the creativity of individuals. Like novels, museums that rest on the imagination of individuals within a nation rather than on the accomplishments of that nation as a whole will be better at portraying its people and the trials they've faced.

The film's director Grant Gee, the director of the !f Istanbul film festival Pelin Turgut, and the director of the Museum of Innocence Onur Karaoğlu are reflected in a green-room mirror prior to the filming of Orhan Pamuk's interview with Grant Gee. February 2016. (From Orhan Pamuk's private collection.)

A Conversation with Grant Gee

ORHAN PAMUK: Welcome, everyone. It all started when Grant Gee came to Istanbul for the screening of his film *Patience (After Sebald)*, based on Sebald's *The Rings of Saturn*. Let's hear about your first take on Istanbul, Grant.

GRANT GEE: I came here knowing nothing, almost nothing about Istanbul beyond a few tourist images in my head.

OP: What were they?

GG: The Blue Mosque . . . I'm sorry!

OP: Did you see that in a movie, Grant?

GG: I had three days and I left the city thinking, 'I have to work here.' It made an impression on me no city ever has in such a short space of time. And then, my wife was actually reading your *Istanbul* and she was telling me, 'You should read this. You would really like this.' And I did. So right from the start, Orhan's vision of Istanbul and my actual experience of Istanbul were mixed up into one thing – they became inseparable.

I returned to England, thinking I had to get back to Istanbul somehow – for a film, for work, anything. I didn't have a plan yet. But then, as if by magic – as these things often go, when you have a strong enough desire, magic starts to happen – I'm reading the *London Review of Books*, and I see a report from the opening night for a thing called the Museum of Innocence, which had just opened in Istanbul. The article says there is something metafictional going on there. Some people who were familiar with the museum started to explain that aspect to me, and within a minute I said, 'Okay, that's the film I want to make.' And then I wrote to Orhan, saying, 'Dear Orhan, please could I make a film about your museum?'

OP: My memory is slightly different, though more or less the same. My agent told me that Grant Gee, who made a film on Sebald's *The Rings of Saturn*, was interested in making a film on the museum and on Istanbul. I watched Grant's film *Patience (After Sebald)* and saw how good a documentary it was. So this was the kind of adaptation he was planning, and I would find myself in the same position as Sebald in that film. I was interested. Coincidentally, I was planning to go to London in November 2012. So we met in London. What was the restaurant where we met?

GG: It was the restaurant of the Royal Institute of British Architects.

OP: As a failed architect who dropped out of architecture school to be a writer, this venue intrigued me. So, we had lunch. What was your impression?

GG: I thought you were going to ask what my lunch was. I think I had a glass of wine – I believe it was a Chardonnay.

OP: You must forgive me, Grant, I have recently had a book published in Turkey and one in Germany, and I've been doing thousands of interviews. All this time I've been waiting for my turn to interview someone famous. It's just your luck that the honour has fallen to you.

GG: I think we got down to business in about ten seconds. You said, 'I liked your Sebald film. If you made a film about my museum and if it was anything like that, I would be happy.'

OP: That's true, we talked about this and that, and there was a moment exactly like you said. But there is one thing you forget, or maybe you are too British and humble to say it. I said to you, 'I loved your film. You are very talented. I'd be very happy if you were to do something similar for me.' It was just as we were saying goodbye, right?

This was October 2012. In December, Grant came to Istanbul. I took you on a long walk – I think from around two o'clock in the afternoon till ten o'clock at night. We walked for eight hours. I would like to talk about that long walk. I picked Grant up and took him first to Nişantaşı, on which enough has already been said, I think. Then from Nişantaşı we went to Osmanbey, Kurtuluş, Pangaltı, Feriköy, Kasımpaşa, and to the neighbourhood of Tarlabaşı, home of Mevlut, the hero of my novel *A Strangeness in My Mind*. We walked, and walked, and walked. I'm sure it will be much more interesting to hear what Grant has to say about that long walk.

GG: I had read in England so many fictional and auto-biographical pieces about Istanbul that it was significant for me to find myself suddenly there, walking around Istanbul with a writer. The thing is, I'm primarily a fan when I make these films. I'm a fan of Orhan's, so I'm still susceptible to the fan thing. I'm like, 'Oh my God, this is a person I'm a fan of, obviously.'

Anyway, you find yourself walking around with him, and it's a slightly weird, fictional experience. You're walking around streets you've been reading about in novels, and then you are able to walk with the person who wrote the novels. So fact and fiction were getting mixed up in my head right from the start. It was a great walk and it was really interesting to understand so much more about the novels that I'd read by doing that. It was especially interesting ending up in Tarlabaşı at about nine o'clock at night, when groups of young men started coming out of the shadows, hissing 'Ssss' and surrounding us. Orhan kept saying, 'Don't worry, don't worry,' and I guess it's common knowledge that Orhan has a bodyguard with him. So we are walking through Tarlabaşı and I'm getting really quite scared because of these quite heavy-looking kids, and it took about ten seconds of quiet conversation with Orhan's bodyguard before these nasty young men all just disappeared again. I still don't know what happened, but it was quite interesting.

OP: Actually, Grant's not telling the whole story. These boys who were trying to sell drugs were suspicious of us, and I had a bodyguard behind me . . .

What next? You returned to London armed with a sense of Istanbul by night, of the visual texture of the city. Meanwhile, during our long walks we had also been negotiating, talking, discussing how to use and adapt the novel, and of course your ideas for this documentary. We had different motivations. We talked about our ideas in coffeehouses and teahouses and as we walked, and while doing so I think we were also negotiating over what each of us wanted to see in the film. Grant had some ideas, I had some ideas, but they were not contradictory. We were very optimistic about this film. So we said, 'We can do this,' and our agents united our ideas in a contract. What were these ideas? What did you want to make, what did I hope you would make? What did the contract say we would make?

GG: For me, the basic idea was to make a film, a poetic documentary that combined elements of objective documentary with the subtleties of what we call, in shorthand, the essay film. So we were going to incorporate some fictional elements. We might have a fictional voice leading the viewer through objective documentary locations and situations.

OP: You said poetic documentary. I'd be happy if you could elaborate on that. There's poetry, and then there's documentary! Surely they are opposites?!

GG: Well . . . My favourite film ever is a film by Chris Marker, *Sans Soleil* – and I think I brought a copy of that movie when I came to meet you.

OP: Yes, we watched this film Grant brought, *Sans Soleil*. You can find it in any shop that sells DVDs of art films, in London, in Paris, or anywhere else. I got myself a copy. It really is a modernist film, or postmodernist, whatever you want to call it – an experimental, dizzying film. Grant, you are a bigger fan than I am, perhaps you'll want to talk about it a little more.

GG: *Sans Soleil* is very simple. It's shot mainly in Japan. The story is that these are shots taken by a fictional cameraman who is meanwhile also writing letters back to a girlfriend of his in France – just saying where he's been, what he's seeing, what he's thinking about. The narration is both funny and sad. He's making comparisons between postmodern societies and simpler societies, he's reflecting on time, memory, and movies he's seen. They are just simple shots of drunks on the street, creatures in a zoo, trees, being on a ferry . . . But out of this, he creates a world that's both factual and fictional.

OP: Since we're on the subject of the influence of other films . . . We haven't yet talked about those influences or precursors whose impact we realised later. While Grant shot, edited, and produced the film, we also had conversations about other films, and other filmmakers whose work interested us. One filmmaker we discussed was Alain Robbe-Grillet. Robbe-Grillet shot a film in Istanbul in the 1960s called *L'Immortelle*. Ömer Kavur, a Turkish director for whom I wrote a script, was an assistant director on that movie. Why that film, and why also Alain Resnais' *L'Année dernière à Marienbad* . . .? Why are these films important to us? Why did we discuss these films and not others? What's the common inspiration behind your film and these sources?

GG: With *L'Année dernière à Marienbad*, it's just because of the tracking shots. I mean, Alain Resnais' tracking shots in the early sixties sort of transformed cinema, into a kind of cinema that was like what the reinventors of a certain type of jazz did: it turned things around. It's the very insistent tracking shots that just keep going without bothering with the niceties of tying things up. This kind of narration gives you a feeling of suspended time and place, the camera puts you into a hypnotic state. That hypnotic, always driving camera was really important.

OP: You've put it very beautifully. But this is not the language of a documentary-maker, by the way. I like your relaxed approach here. So this background was more or less our inspiration for our film; just walking on the street doesn't guarantee you'll end up with a good film.

Let's talk about what was written in our contract. After our first meeting and our conversations as we both walked around Istanbul, you came to Istanbul again in the summer of 2013, this time to Büyükada, and again we walked and talked and chatted. We weren't sightseeing this time, but discussing the structure of the film.

GG: About the narrator, and about other things . . . It was all very well to have these interesting formal techniques to play with, but what's going to make this film human? I liked what you said about *Sans Soleil*: 'It's a very interesting film, but if we make a film like this, there are going to be five people in the audience, and three of them will walk out.'

OP: I didn't just love that film, I combed through it – I'd watch for ten seconds and then go off to google things for two hours, trying to understand, before resuming where I left off . . .

GG: So that's what we were talking about: 'How do we make the museum, Istanbul, and the novel into a movie?' Right from the start you were understandably more concerned, more interested in how we were going to make this material into a movie. How do we make this a movie that people are going to enjoy?

OP: I was probably having one of my internal conflicts: I wanted to be extremely experimental, but I wanted people to enjoy my experimentality, two wishes which were contradictory by definition. But maybe we could find a solution. So we kept talking. We started filming on the streets we had walked on, and meanwhile continued to walk.

Making an experimental film like *Sans Soleil* is interesting in its own right, but we also wanted there to be some plot, a storyline, something like that. And we were also interested in the idea that the Museum of Innocence was both a novel and a museum, weren't we?

Then you said, 'Well, who's going to tell the story? Who's going to talk here? This is a documentary after all.' The main characters from *The Museum of Innocence*, Kemal and Füsun, were already dead. So what were we going to do? Then one of us, I can't remember which, had an idea.

GG: I think it was me.

OP: Ah yes, that's what I was about to say. The secret's out now!

GG: Thank you. So who was going to be the narrator? If you are going to do something formally experimental, then to have a single voice holding it together – a voice which is engaging – is very important. Generally, essay films – though not *Sans Soleil* – are narrated by men. Because of the kind of sexual politics explored in the museum and the novel, I thought it could be interesting to have a woman as the voice. Because . . . just, because. So, who's this woman? I had really liked *The Black Book* – the detective story. So maybe there could be some kind of detective thing, this woman looking for traces of Füsun . . .

OP: Yes, although this idea is not so prominent in the movie because I was reluctant to go too much into the subject of Füsun's apparent suicide. You had in mind someone coming along years later, researching Füsun's death. Was it a suicide, or a death caused by societal pressures, as in *Anna Karenina*? Or had Kemal killed her? I don't believe that, and in fact I never thought of going down that route. Meanwhile, we began developing a different idea, which ultimately led us to find Ayla.

Ayla is a secondary character in the novel. The novel has an index. If you have a copy of the book at home, you can check the index and you will see that Ayla is definitely in the story. We decided to use her, because Kemal is dead and Füsun is dead. And we mustn't forget that Grant wanted to see today's Istanbul, the Istanbul of the last fifteen years: high-rises, new buildings . . . Those of you who have seen the film will have noticed that its texture, its architectural Istanbul is not the Istanbul of my novel *The Museum of Innocence*, but a vision of today's Istanbul. Grant wanted to do a film that was (a) partly about the Museum of Innocence, (b) on my work, (c) on Istanbul, and (d) on today's Istanbul. I was supposed to come up with a solution. The solution was Ayla. These prescriptions also indicated what Ayla's story should be. She would have had to leave Istanbul for a while, some time after the deaths of Füsun and Kemal, and be surprised upon her return by Istanbul's immeasurable development over the last ten years: high-rises, everything being demolished, houses being destroyed. Grant wanted these things in the film too, so we invented Ayla.

GG: To be honest, Ayla was all his work.

OP: I must admit I was a little worried at this stage because I have always thought that the Istanbul of *The Museum of Innocence* is very close to the Istanbul of the sixties, seventies, eighties described in my autobiographical book *Istanbul: Memories and the City* – not to today's Istanbul of high-rises. How was he going to make this work? While I kept dragging him into more historic neighbourhoods that dramatise and illustrate the city, Grant kept going to new neighbourhoods. I would think, 'Don't go there! What's there to see?'

GG: What I knew as someone who had put together films before, working in my own singular way, was that as long as you've got the voice that does the work at the front, then all sorts of visual things can be going on in the background without conflict. So the voice can be talking about this and that while you're walking underneath a subway bridge in 2005. As long as the voice is bringing everything together, you can go with the voice first, and the pictures will add an interesting harmony to it all. But the voice doesn't always help. So once Orhan agreed to write the script, I had this idea that the voice should be Ayla's. She goes away, she comes back again. This made me feel very free with the visuals, which is a great way to be.

OP: In a way I lived with Ayla, just like I had lived in *My Name Is Red* and *Snow*. I was also conscious that both of those novels have a character who is absent from Istanbul and returns after twelve years. Now, again, I had a character who comes back to Istanbul after twelve years. Ayla would return to her hometown after twelve years and, faced with its transformation, she would think, 'My God, how it has changed!' In *My Name Is Red*, the character Black (*Kara*) returns to the city and sees how much it has changed. In *Snow* too there is a character who is absent from Istanbul in a similar way. In both cases, it is for a period of twelve years. Ayla leaves Istanbul because her husband has some political problems, so they go to Bremen for a while, before coming back. Ayla is both startled and upset by the new high-rises, the development of new neighbourhoods.

Grant, I think you'll want to talk about an important stage in our development of the film: the contract. The contract my agent and his agent concluded said, more or less, that Grant Gee is going to make a film based on Pamuk's book and his vision of Istanbul. He would be free to quote from any of my books – he was particularly interested in *The Black Book*, *Istanbul*, and *The Museum of Innocence* – and he might edit these excerpts slightly to make them sound as if they came from Ayla's mouth. Meanwhile, I would write a script of about thirty minutes, creating Ayla's monologue. I also agreed to do a long interview with someone for Grant to use in the film. At that stage, having sorted out the contract and fulfilled my contractual duties – writing a new text, doing an interview, and helping Grant out whenever he came here, showing him around – I thought, 'Well, it's not my film, it's his. God be with him.'

GG: Yes, the interview provided a really interesting angle on things. I was walking around Istanbul – if you've seen the film you know this – and what I didn't want was to end up with an ordinary moving, poetic film about Istanbul because when you do that what you get is a full-screen talking head going blah blah blah, and it just flattens the whole film. The question is how to integrate talking-head material. It's great stuff, the interview, but these days, especially when documentary filmmakers are trying to be more cinematic all the time, if you put in just the interview on a full screen, people think, 'Eeeh, I'd rather watch TV, you know, why am I sitting here, why am I paying twenty euros to see this?'

Going back to the interview with Orhan: as I was walking around Istanbul late at night, thinking about this film, I saw that in all the shops here you have those little TVs always running in the back. And I thought, 'Okay, this is interesting.' I wondered if any of these guys watched arts programmes. And I asked Orhan if there was any Turkish arts programme that had done an interview with him. That would have been really good. And Orhan said there really were programmes like that, so I said, 'Great, we'll make one, too!' It was really interesting. It didn't all end up in the film. It was actually a three-hour interview with Orhan in a studio with three cameras and the writer Emre Ayvaz. We even had a title sequence, end credits – in short, we made a proper programme. I can't remember the name in Turkish, but in English it was 'Witness'. Then we played the recording of the interview on TVs and filmed as we walked past them. That was how we managed to integrate the talking heads you find in conventional documentaries into our creative universe. It was a good solution.

OP: If I remember correctly, we weren't always planning a ninety-minute feature film. But we ended up with a normal full-length film. Grant started off making a documentary that would be maybe forty minutes long. The people who were financing the film had intended it for TV. The idea that the film might end up screened in movie theatres, at the Venice

Film Festival, the !f Festival, or some festival in Paris seemed only a flight of fancy. We weren't really thinking along those lines; it was never in our plans. We were reluctant to even dream about it. The idea that we might actually make a full-length feature film only came later. But really we only set off thinking we'd make a modest documentary.

GG: It's one way of making odd documentary films, slightly unconventional documentary films. It can be five minutes long, it can be ten minutes long, but you have to find something that can push and sustain you through the process. As it gets bigger, it only feels better. But whether you're working for TV or for the internet, the basic impulse is to aspire to something good.

OP: We have come to the most interesting question, I think: what is an unconventional documentary?

GG: I don't think there are any conventional documentaries left any more. I don't know about here, but in England, as TV has become more purely entertainment-based, all those documentary filmmakers who used to make fifteen programmes for broadcast on the country's main TV channels are now out of a job. So what they are forced to do now is to go to the people who finance films and say, 'I have an idea for cinema: a documentary!' We got our main funding from the British Film Institute. The first time we talked about this project with them, they said, 'Until two years ago, we used to get 300 applications a year to make feature-length documentary films. Now we get 2,500.' That's because everybody now is saying, 'My documentary is a movie.' They have bigger production values, cute ideas, and more fiction is brought into it. It's a way of getting your films made. So the lines between what is a fiction feature and what is a documentary feature are starting to get very blurred.

OP: This seems not unlike the developments in postmodernist history during the 1980s and 1990s. A good example may be Simon Schama, who was then a professor of art history at Harvard and doing historical research on some event in American history. He had done enough research to write an academic book in the classic sense. But Schama threw caution to the wind and wrote a novel instead. Bear in mind this was the era of high postmodernism. He took all his knowledge of social patterns and of the history of art, making little changes to certain details, but with a precision befitting a professor, and wrote *Dead Certainties: Unwarranted Speculations*, published in 1991. This was both a novel and the novelistic experiment of a respected historian. But I'm very curious to learn about what you've just said: to make an entertaining documentary, you must make it fictional.

GG: So we were at another meeting where the eventual producers told us they liked our idea, that they were interested in putting money into this film because, they said, 'It is going to be a cinematic documentary, and when the 2,500 directors who are sending us their ideas ask "What do you mean, a cinematic documentary?", we'll be able to say, "Something like this."' I hadn't realised Simon Schama had done that, and suddenly that's opening up all sorts of things – I'm thinking of the anthropologist Marc Augé, who wrote a book that was really influential for filmmakers of my generation called *Non-Places*.

OP: I think the beginning of the whole thing was the surrealists' relationship with anthropologists during the 1930s. The surrealists were influenced by anthropology and the social sciences, and some of these social scientists were using surrealism as a form of expression. But this was dangerous territory and things could easily slide into racism: the 1930s surrealists were inclined to approach the idea of natives/savages, which was a topic of anthropological investigation, from a racist, exoticising angle. Anyway, for a time, the social sciences went hand in hand with fiction, the creative arts, and surrealism. Your film is an example of this kind of thing. It is both a documentary and a work of fiction. Would you say that your film based on *The Rings of Saturn* was also like this?

GG: Yes.

OP: My answer would be: 'In a visual sense, yes!'

GG: Yes, it was. But with Sebald, the fiction is in the way he overlays history onto what's in front of his eyes. So his fiction is a combination of a real place and something half remembered, maybe something with an element of falsehood in it. This creates an uncanny atmosphere, which again goes back to surrealism, and so on.

OP: So you started shooting your movie. I was telling my close friends at this time, 'Well, it's his film, I won't interfere.' But at the same time I was betraying that statement by being curious, by trying to control the process . . . I saw you doing interviews with Türkan Şoray and Ara Güler, and becoming infatuated with the things you were discovering in Istanbul, and I got a bit upset. But maybe we can come to that later.

GG: Well, when the 'talent' – and in this case, drama is the talent, the lead actor – when the talent starts getting a bit jumpy about what the director is planning, the director has to draw on resources deep inside himself to keep the core of the film in his line of sight. I just knew that what I had in mind was the right thing to do. I would listen to Orhan's objections, some of which were right, some of which weren't, and I would think, 'It's okay, just keep going.' It's really difficult because you can collaborate with people, and talk to people every step of the way, but even people who work in the film industry, people I've been working with for years and years and years, know that when you are shooting and when you are editing a film, when it's not been made yet, nobody actually knows what's going on apart from the director. Even the editors right there with you don't quite understand. And so all people have is their own taste, and their own fears and anxieties, that they project onto the thing. One of the hardest things about directing is when the people around you start getting anxious. This usually happens halfway through a shoot, or halfway through the edit. Everyone's anxieties start raining down: 'What is this? This isn't what I thought it would be . . .' and the like. Of course, you have to listen to what's being said if it's a genuine concern. But you always tell yourself, 'I know this is going to work out okay.'

OP: Don't worry, Grant. We had some stormy times, but our marriage has survived.

Anyway, while he was happy with his experimentalism, I was worried – about what was happening to my book, my life, my story at that time.

GG: I was filming Türkan Şoray around that time.

OP: Yes, Türkan Şoray especially. 'Why is Türkan Şoray here?' I would ask. 'She's in *The Black Book*, isn't she?' Grant would reply. Until finally, the film was finished.

I'm very happy with the film. I enjoyed watching it. I also think it's an intellectual film. It's a heavy, dense film. It's not a popularised, sugar-coated version of my novel *The Museum of Innocence*. It's a serious film, a film with its own visual universe. I'm proud that there is such a beautiful film based on my writing and, of course, on the director's imagination. It's Grant's film completely. I only worked as a scriptwriter during its production.

GG: It's one of those geeky cinephile and filmmaker things: it all goes back to the fact/fiction divide. What's factual and what's fictional filmmaking? I think it was probably Godard who said that 'cinema comes from two sources'. One of the sources is Lumière – you know, the train arriving at the station without blocking off the camera, as if it were real. And then there is the Méliès source, Georges Méliès' *Le Voyage dans la lune*. That is a twin birth in cinema. They are two completely different strands: the Lumière strand is pure objectivity, and Méliès is the visionary strand. That opposition, and the result of that twin birth, have never been clear.

OP: Where do we stand with regards to these strands?

GG: We are somewhere in-between. There has always been a line, a scale between those two things. You are never entirely Lumière or Méliès, you are always . . . any film is always somewhere on the line between those two points. Never purely one or the other. And that takes us back to the origins of cinema.

OP: I agree with you on this point.

You know, I've always wanted to see what goes on in a film studio, but of course it was impossible because you were working back home in England. All the material in a studio, all those buttons, screens, and control mechanisms, in my mind I've always pictured it like a cockpit. I've always thought that operating this technical equipment must be like piloting a plane. Could you tell us more about what you do in a studio?

GG: I mean, for the editing our blessing for the past fifteen years has been one piece of kit, which is Apple's Final Cut Pro. And they don't pay me to say that, I've always paid them, despite the fact that they have betrayed us so many times and have become something of a Big Brother.

It's one piece of very good editing software. You have all these tracks, all these different layers. So that's why we use this editing software. But whereas usually people have one track with two or four or six soundtracks, we must have had twenty-four audio tracks, and about eight layers of video stacked up. If you see a picture of the timeline – we always take photographs of the timeline when the project is completed – it looks like a city: all the tracks are stacked up like skyscrapers, rather than just a single line.

OP: When you say 'my editor', who is this person? Are they in the room with you all the time, or . . .

GG: The relationship is like that of a 'work wife'. Each

marriage is different. I've been working with this guy for twenty years, and what I generally do is I do a very rough cut to block out the sort of thing that's not working on certain scenes. And there's this mess all over the computer, and he comes in and he's like, 'Oh, really?' and spends months and months cutting and tidying up and making it flow. He's a musician as well, he's responsible for that kind of thing – he's very tidy, very particular, he cares about musicality. So he gives this thing its fine form. He sculpts it.

OP: I was very curious about how all these images, the narration, the music all intertwined so gloriously. I thought it was you who had done it.

GG: I do the demo. I play the guitar and sing. And he makes it into a fine thing.

OP: I remember during one of these periods when you were working, sometimes I got to see what you were doing, and you would say things like, 'My God, I'm working so hard.' What did you mean by that?

GG: It's very difficult because there's no storyboard. There's a pile of material. And you have to draw a line through all this material – not just to make sense of it, but to make something compelling, emotional, all the things you want in a movie. But what you've got is walking around Istanbul at night, some old movies, pictures of objects in the museum, and an interview with a writer. Try making something compelling out of that. It's really hard. I've been doing this for twenty-five years now, and it's still really hard to make something good, or even half good.

OP: Well, we are grateful to you for this wonderful film. Now we have to wait and see how Turkish audiences are going to react to it. That's why we're here. After the film is released, we will see the response and decide how to use the film in the museum. Of course, this will involve copyright issues, negotiations, things like that . . . Anyway, I think Grant is pleased, too.

GG: The first thing that really grabbed me about Orhan's writing was the passage in *Istanbul* about *hüzün*. I've thought a lot about why I connected with this, especially as it's so much about everyday street scenes in Istanbul. I decided that the connection between someone talking about their experiences in Istanbul in the 1960s, seventies, eighties and my experience was that I grew up in a very provincial part of Britain, and through the late 1960s and early seventies I always wanted to be somewhere else, nearer to the centre of life, like Orhan's characters. Everyone else wanted the same. All our clubs seemed kind of cheap. All our cars seemed kind of cheap. Everyone seemed gloomy and I really wanted to be like an American living in America, where things were more colourful. I think it was this universal sense of being provincial that really touched me. Orhan wrote about a nation, the national feeling of provincialism. Anyone can feel they are not at the centre of things. It's one of those universal feelings, almost.

OP: A universal sentiment.

GG: Yes, one of those universal sentiments. It wasn't always a literary thing that I felt. Especially because we are working from translations, so you are always aware you are not quite up against the language that the writer really wants to use. It's always somehow diffused. So you are always having to make an additional interpretative effort. But that was really the first thing that got me, it was as if we were two provincial painters, and that was remarkable. I grew up in a provincial part of England and somehow, through literature, I was able to make an emotional connection to Turkey.

OP: Thank you, Grant, and thank you all for being here and for your kind questions.